POLITICAL
PARTIES
MATTER

POLITICAL PARTIES MATTER

Realignment and the Return of Partisan Voting

Jeffrey M. Stonecash

LYNNE
RIENNER
PUBLISHERS

BOULDER
LONDON

Published in the United States of America in 2006 by
Lynne Rienner Publishers, Inc.
1800 30th Street, Boulder, Colorado 80301
www.rienner.com

and in the United Kingdom by
Lynne Rienner Publishers, Inc.
3 Henrietta Street, Covent Garden, London WC2E 8LU

Library of Congress Cataloging-in-Publication Data
Stonecash, Jeffrey M.
    Political parties matter : realignment and the return of partisan voting /
Jeffrey M. Stonecash.
    Includes bibliographical references and index.
    ISBN 1-58826-369-X (hardcover : alk. paper)
    ISBN 1-58826-394-0 (pbk : alk. paper)
    1. Party affiliation—United States.   2. Party affiliation—United
States—History.   3. Political parties—United States.   4. Political
Parties—United States—History.   5. Voting—United States.   6.
Voting—United States—History.   I. Title.
JK2261.S863   2005
324.273—dc22

                                                        2005018291

British Cataloguing in Publication Data
A Cataloguing in Publication record for this book
is available from the British Library.

Printed and bound in the United States of America

 The paper used in this publication meets the requirements
of the American National Standard for Permanence of
Paper for Printed Library Materials Z39.48-1992.

5   4   3   2   1

To Lindsay, Cassie, and Maggie

Contents

Preface

The attachment of people to political parties is changing, and in ways we did not expect several years ago. In the 1960s, evidence began to accumulate that electoral attachments to the parties were declining. Fewer people identified themselves in surveys as Democrats or Republicans. Those who did identify with a party were less inclined to vote for candidates of "their" party. More voters were splitting their tickets between House and presidential candidates of differing parties. Split outcomes in House districts increased, as did situations in which the party winning the House race and the presidential party vote in a district differed. The evidence seemed clear that partisanship was declining in importance, and that parties were becoming less central to US politics.

Further, there was a very plausible explanation of why partisanship was declining in importance. The fundamental issue of whether government should provide some sort of "safety net" for those experiencing economic problems seemed to have been resolved in the affirmative. Real incomes had grown from 1945 to 1970, and class divisions were seen to be declining as economic issues faded in relevance. Perhaps more significant, the inclination and capability of candidates to diminish the role of partisan attachments were apparently increasing.

More members of Congress wanted to stay in office, and more were staying longer. They sought to establish more personal and stable electoral bases and to diminish the impact of national issues and partisan swings in electoral voting that could put them out of office. They had access to more official resources of office—staff, computers, mail—with which to present themselves to voters, respond to problems, and curry favor. They were raising more campaign funds. They had access to pollsters who could track their district standing and warn them of electoral problems. A growing pool of consultants could create campaign ads to boost candidates' visibility and scare away challengers. The combination of better information, more staff resources, and more campaign funds allowed incumbents to create a "personal" vote, reducing the impact of partisanship in US politics. Campaigns were seen as "candidate-centered," not party-centered.

Then, in the 1990s, the trends in partisanship reversed. The same indicators that had suggested a decline in the attachment of voters to parties and in partisan voting behavior indicated that partisanship was increasing. There was no discernible change in the motives or behaviors of politicians, but the indicators of partisanship began to steadily increase. Parties once again were central to voters and to politicians.

The shift of the last decade or so prompts several fundamental questions about partisanship. Why did partisanship decline in the 1960s and 1970s, and what did that decline reflect? Were we in fact witnessing the decline of parties, or was some other trend playing out? What made the trends reverse? And in light of that reversal, what do we make of the argument that campaigns and elections are candidate-centered?

My argument in this book is that the trends in partisanship of the last fifty years reflect the consequences of a long-term secular realignment. The parties have undergone a gradual and steady re-sorting of electoral bases. As the electorate reacted to these changes, it created the appearance of a movement away from parties—but these changes were really a reflection of the transitions associated with realignment. Although my immediate concern is trends in partisanship, the broader concern is the role of realignment and the current party polarization that has emerged in US politics.

POLITICAL
PARTIES
MATTER

1

The Puzzling Reemergence of Partisanship

The Formation of a Consensus

Until the last decade, there was an apparent consensus that the electorate's attachment to political parties was declining. There was clear and pervasive evidence that voters were less tied to parties. The first evidence emerged at the aggregate level and traced a historical pattern of declining "party" voting. Burnham (1965) using aggregate data from states or House districts, documented a rise in split-ticket voting from the early 1900s through the 1960s. The percentage of House districts in which the partisan outcome for the presidential and House vote differed was steadily increasing (Jones, 1964: 465; Cummings, 1966: 31–39), and the correlation between partisan voting percentages for House and presidential candidates across House districts was declining (Burnham, 1975: 428). In 1900, less than 5 percent of districts had a House and presidential winner from different parties. The vote for the president was virtually the same as that for House candidates of the same party. By 1972, however, 44 percent of House districts had divided partisan outcomes. The percentage of districts with these "split outcomes" kept rising through the 1970s (Burden and Kimball, 2002: 5).

At the individual level, the evidence confirmed the trend that voters were less attached to parties. Studies using the National Election Studies surveys of individuals provided evidence that from 1952 through the 1970s there was an increase in the percentage of voters defining themselves as independents rather than partisans (i.e., a Democrat or a Republican) (Converse, 1976: 32, 70; Nie et al., 1976: 47; Crotty, 1984: 26–37). Those who said they identified with a party were less inclined to vote for the candidates of that party. Split-ticket voting, or voting for one party's candidate for president, and another party's candidate for the House, was increasing (Nie et al., 1976: 47–73; Flanigan and Zingale, 1979: 45–60). Wattenberg (1990) found that fewer and fewer respondents could name anything they liked or disliked about parties, and he concluded that we had moved into a new world of "candidate-centered politics" (Wattenberg, 1991).

This general decline in partisanship through the 1970s fit with a view that the old antagonisms and sources of political division were declining and that there was less reason for voters to be strongly attached to parties. Class divisions were seen as declining, such that the great issues of economic fairness and the obligation of government to address inequality were less salient as a source of party attachments (Ladd and Hadley, 1975; Inglehart, 1971, 1977, 1997; Stonecash, 2000: 141–158). American politics had reached an "end of ideology," with many of the great issues presumably less divisive because of an emerging consensus about the role of government (Bell, 1962, 1973). The great issues of politics—whether government should help people and whether it should intrude into the private sector—which might rouse voters and lead them to join one party over another, seemed resolved. These issues had been displaced by more emotional and volatile cultural issues—crime, affirmative action, abortion, free speech—which provided less of a stable basis for dividing voters (Edsall and Edsall, 1991; Leege et al., 2002).

The parties had also gradually lost some of their mechanisms to influence politics and mobilize the electorate. The Progressive movement had been successful in creating the direct primary, which reduced the ability of party leaders to control nominations (Ware, 2002). Reformers also were able to institute civil service, reducing the number of patronage positions and the number of faithful party workers (Hofstader, 1955; Hays, 1964). Advance registration was instituted, making it more difficult to mobilize large numbers of voters in a relatively short time before elections. The combination of a decline in issue conflict and parties with fewer mechanisms to mobilize voters created a diminished basis for intense partisan divisions and attachments.

As the issue basis of divisions declined during the 1960s and 1970s, those seeking to influence voting were also seen as acting differently. Politicians, the central actors in this process, were seen as more concerned with repressing partisanship and with developing a personal image and following that was separate from partisan divisions. Mayhew

(1974a, 1974b) posited the simple assumption that the primary goal of members of Congress was reelection. The argument was that members now had more access to resources to create a personal vote to keep them in office. They could now promote their own visibility and identity and separate their image from that of their party, allowing them to become more independent of partisan swings in the nation (Jacobson, 2001: 21–40). The result would be a candidate-centered politics, as distinct from a party-centered politics. The result would be a decline in attachment to parties among voters.

There was considerable evidence to support the view that politicians were somehow different. An increasing percentage of legislators at the state (Stonecash, 1993) and national levels (Polsby, 1968) were running for reelection. More and more legislators at both levels were succeeding in staying in office longer. With congressional members having longer careers, more elected officials were seeking to diminish the impact of partisan voting.

Politicians were also acquiring greater access to the resources that would allow them to exploit this situation. Incumbents in the House during the 1960s and 1970s were allocating themselves more perks of office (e.g., staff and mailing budgets), which allowed them to increase their visibility (Mayhew, 1974a; Jacobson, 2001: 21–100). These resources can be used to respond to constituency needs, to advertise the presence and accomplishments of members through newsletters and mailings, and to schedule appearances at local meetings (Mayhew, 1974b: 306–313; Jacobson, 2001: 21–55).

Incumbents could also exploit their positions to raise money from those interested in the progress of legislation, providing them with more resources to present themselves to voters through direct mail and media ads. The emergence of television made it easier for candidates to present themselves and change votes (Shively, 1992). During the 1970s, campaign expenditures were increasing (Campaign Finance Institute, 2002), giving incumbents more ability to utilize political polling, direct mail, and radio and television ads to promote their personal images. All these resources (public budgets and privately raised funds) allowed incumbents to raise their margins of victory and create high reelection rates in the House, distancing their electoral fortunes from those of presidential candidates. It was unclear whether declining electoral attachments to parties came first or candidate activities created the trend, but the interpretation of declining attachment to parties and the evidence of this all supported a view that candidate-centered politics had displaced campaigns focused on political parties (Herrnson, 1998; Menefee-Libey, 2000). Candidates were creating personal and less partisan images with voters, resulting in unique and varying electoral bases.

Voting results suggested that House candidates were succeeding in distancing themselves from the vote for their presidential candidates. There was less and less of an association in House districts between the vote for a House candidate of one party and that for the presidential vote of the same party. Figures 1.1 and 1.2 indicate how much change in voting habits had occurred since the beginning of the century. The figures plot, by House district, the percentage won by the Democratic presidential candidate versus the percentage won by the House Democratic candidate (see Appendix B for an explanation of the data).[1] In 1900, a strong relationship existed between the two, such that the vote for one office coincided with the vote for the other. By 1972, the relationship had "come apart." The presidential vote was not strongly associated with the vote for House candidates. The Democratic presidential candidate might get 40 percent, while House candidates might receive anywhere from 25 to 100 percent. The correlation between the vote for House and presidential candidates was clearly declining. A high correlation indicates that the vote across districts is very similar, where-

Figure 1.1   Scatterplot of Vote Percentages Within House Districts for Democratic House and Presidential Candidates, 1900

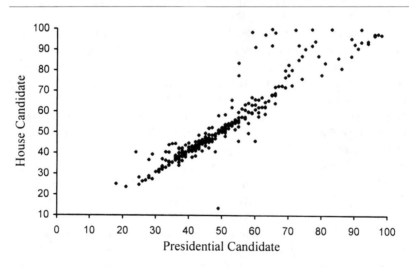

Source: Data compiled by author. See Appendix B for an explanation.

Figure 1.2　Scatterplot of Vote Percentages Within House Districts for Democratic House and Presidential Candidates, 1972

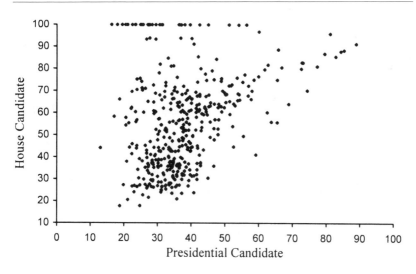

Source: Data compiled by author. See Appendix B for an explanation.

as a low correlation indicates that the votes are largely independent of each other. That correlation was consistently above 0.90 for the first half of the 1900s (Cummings, 1966: 31–39), but had declined to 0.20 by 1972.

If incumbents were able to exploit this situation, their success at achieving reelection should have been rising. The evidence indeed indicated that incumbents were increasingly successful in retaining office but that this increase only roughly coincided with the allocation of more resources to members of Congress. A major increase in congressional resources for members (e.g., staff, office budgets for mailings, trips home for members) occurred after 1946. From 1946 through the 1970s, the reelection rates of House and Senate members had gradually, if somewhat erratically, risen. Figure 1.3 indicates the percentage of incumbents seeking reelection in each year who won. Incumbent reelection rates began to rise in the late 1880s (Benjamin and Malbin, 1992: 291–293), and that increase continued through the 1900s. It was very plausible that something such as greater access to the resources that help reelection efforts was transforming election outcomes and making it easier for incumbents to win.

Figure 1.3   Congressional Reelection Rates for Incumbents Seeking Reelection, 1790–2002

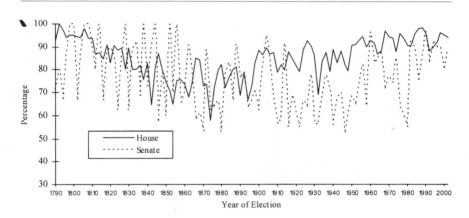

Sources: Gerald Benjamin and Michael J. Malbin, *Limiting Legislative Terms* (Washington, D.C.: Congressional Quarterly Press, 1992), pp. 291–293, and data compiled by the author.

Studies also found that the percentage of the vote received by incumbents was increasing. The assumption was that incumbents had found ways to increase their normal advantage over challengers, and considerable attention was devoted to the nature of the "incumbency advantage," or the ability of incumbents to raise their vote proportion above what might normally prevail in a district.[2] Winning incumbents in contested races received an average vote percentage of 61.1 from 1946 to 1964 and during the period 1966–1980, the average increased to 64.3. The rise of both reelection rates and vote percentages suggested that the electoral process was being transformed.

All in all, the data seemed fairly convincing that the attachment of voters to parties and the impact of party identification on voting were declining (Keith et al., 1992: 1–22; Fiorina, 2002: 99–103). The evidence at the aggregate and individual levels led to the same conclusion. By the mid-1970s, Nie et al. (1976: 47) concluded, "Perhaps the most dramatic change in the American public over the past two decades has been the decline of partisanship." Books with titles such as *The Party's Over* (Broder, 1972) and *American Parties in Decline* (Crotty, 1984) were common, confirming the decline of parties and partisanship. It appeared that a fundamental change in attachment to parties had occurred by the 1970s.

The Resurgence of Partisanship

While this interpretation was developing, something unexpected occurred. The trends providing the supporting evidence for the interpretation reversed. Since the 1990s, the evidence indicates an increasing attachment to parties. The changes are evident at both the aggregate and individual levels.

At the aggregate level, the two important indicators of partisan voting are the presence of split outcomes and the correlation between House and presidential outcomes. Figure 1.4 presents the trends of these two indicators for the last century. From 1900 to 1952, the percentage of House districts in which differing parties won these two contests was usually below 20 percent. Beginning in 1944, this percentage began to steadily rise, and for 1956–1988 the percentage averaged 33.4.

Figure 1.4   The Association of House–Presidential Results: Correlation and Split Outcomes, 1900–2000

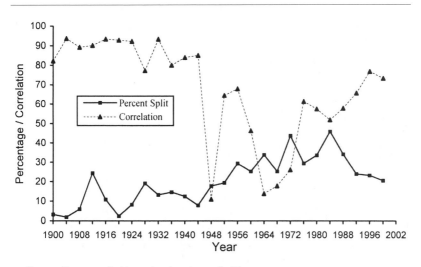

Source: Data compiled by author (see Appendix B).

Notes: Percentages are expressed as ranging from 0 to 100, and correlations are rescaled to range from 0 to 100 rather than 0 to 1. A district is defined as having a split outcome when the party winning the House contest is different from that winning the presidential vote within the district. Those districts for which the presidential vote is not known, from 1900 to 1948, are not included. The missing scores involve counties with multiple districts within them (e.g., Cook County in Illinois, New York City, and Suffolk County in Massachusetts). Data on outcomes for these counties have never been collected and disaggregated (see Appendix B).

Then this percentage began to decline, and for 1992–2000, the percentage averaged 22.7. The correlation of House and presidential votes within House districts follows a pattern of declining and then rising in recent years. From 1900 to 1944, this correlation was very high. It then dropped dramatically in 1948, came back up, but then dropped again until 1964. Since then, this correlation has steadily increased. Both indicators of district-level results point to a return of partisanship.

Individual-level data also indicate a resurgence of partisanship. The collection of consistent survey data began in 1952, and these data indicate a long-term pattern of decline and then renewed partisanship. Table 1.1 provides time-series data on several indicators of individual attachment to parties. The data, drawn from the National Election Study (NES) Cumulative Data File, 1948–2002, indicate trends since 1952 for the percentage of the electorate identifying as independents, the percentage of voters who identify with a party but vote for a candidate of the other party, and split-ticket voting. Almost all the indicators follow the same pattern over time. Disengagement from parties began to rise in the late 1960s and early 1970s, peaked during the 1970s and 1980s, and then declined during the 1990s. To more easily track broad changes, the yearly results are grouped and averaged within each decade at the bottom of Table 1.1. For all indicators, except for those choosing independent when initially asked their party identification, the percentages in the 1990s and the 2000s are lower than the corresponding percentages in the 1970s and 1980s.

The party attachments of voters are increasingly associated with race (Carmines and Stimson, 1989); religious views (Layman, 2001); class (Stonecash, 2000); and ideology (Abramowitz, 1994; Abramowitz and Saunders, 1998). Voters who differ on these traits also differ on the parties they support. This decline and resurgence of partisanship is also reflected in Congress (Jacobson, 2003a). In the 1950s, Democrats in Congress were relatively unified in voting together and against Republicans, who in turn voted together and against Democrats. These partisan divisions declined during the 1960s and 1970s and then began to increase in the 1980s and 1990s. The parties are now divided across a broad array of issues (Bond and Fleisher, 2000; Stonecash et al., 2002).

Reassessing the Evidence of Partisan Decline

A trend of declining partisanship seemed clear in the 1970s and for much of the 1980s, but the evidence now indicates that that conclusion

Table 1.1   Individual Indicators of Party Disengagement: Independents, Voting Defections from Party, and Split-Ticket Voting

Year	Percent Independent[a] Initial (1)	Without leaners (2)	Percentage of Partisans Voting for Party Candidate of Other Party[b] Pres. (3)	Senate (4)	House (5)	Percentage of Partisans Voting Split-Ticket[c] P – H (6)	P – S (7)
1952	23.3	5.8	17.8	14.0	12.5	12.2	11.8
1954	22.7	7.3					
1956	24.4	8.8	16.3	11.0	10.1	13.3	13.0
1958	19.7	7.1		9.5	10.1		
1960	21.7	9.2	15.9	15.0	12.1	12.8	12.8
1962	22.1	7.8			9.8		
1964	23.0	7.8	16.5	14.8	15.0	14.7	15.8
1966	28.7	12.3		16.3	15.1		
1968	29.5	10.5	14.9	17.4	18.2	16.0	13.8
1970	31.3	12.9		11.8	14.8		
1972	35.2	13.1	27.1	23.0	17.1	28.0	24.7
1974	36.4	13.7		17.4	17.6		
1976	35.8	14.1	15.9	18.6	19.3	21.7	17.4
1978	38.5	13.7		20.1	21.0		
1980	35.3	12.9	15.9	19.4	23.3	25.3	20.2
1982	30.6	11.1		17.2	16.8		
1984	34.8	11.0	13.8	19.0	22.2	21.4	18.9
1986	33.5	11.5		20.0	20.7		
1988	36.3	10.6	12.4	19.9	20.0	22.1	20.3
1990	35.3	10.4		20.6	18.4		
1992	38.7	11.6	9.6	19.5	19.9	19.5	18.6
1994	34.8	10.0		16.4	15.3		
1996	33.1	8.5	8.5	13.5	15.8	15.0	10.6
1998	35.1	10.0		15.7	19.6		
2000	39.7	11.5	6.4	11.3	15.5	15.4	11.6
2002	33.3	6.9		11.3	15.4		

Decade Averages[d]

Year	Initial (1)	Without leaners (2)	Pres. (3)	Senate (4)	House (5)	P – H (6)	P – S (7)
1950s	22.5	7.3	17.1	11.5	11.3	12.8	12.4
1960s	25.0	9.5	15.8	15.9	16.1	14.5	14.1
1970s	35.4	13.5	21.5	18.2	18.0	24.9	21.1
1980s	34.1	11.4	14.0	19.1	20.6	23.0	19.8
1990s	35.4	10.1	9.1	17.1	17.8	17.3	14.6
2000s	36.5	9.2	6.4	11.3	15.5	15.4	11.6

Source: NES Cumulative Data File, 1948–2002.

Notes:

a. Two percentages are used. Column (1) is the percentage of those choosing independent when first asked about their party identification. For column (2), those leaning to a party when asked in a follow-up question have been moved to the identifying category.

b. Columns (3)–(5) indicate the percentages of those *initially* defining themselves as Democrats or Republicans (vcf0301) who voted for the presidential candidate of the other party.

c. Columns (6) and (7) indicate the percentage of those voting for a presidential (P) and a House (H or S) candidate of different parties.

d. Decade averages are averages of years, not pooled results within a decade.

was premature. Even though the most recent trends cover only 10 to 15 years, they clearly indicate that partisanship is now increasing. These patterns are the opposite of what we expect if partisanship is declining and candidates are able to create a political process that is focused on themselves and not parties.

Other evidence points to the need to reconsider the argument that partisanship is waning. The candidate-centered framework for interpreting politics emerged as part of the effort to explain why the vote percentage of incumbents increased after 1946 (Mayhew, 1974a, 1974b; Jacobson, 2001: 26). This apparent increase was taken as evidence that incumbents could get voters to vote for them as incumbents and not just for their party affiliation. Why this increase was occurring became central to the study of congressional elections.

The difficulty is that evidence indicates that there was no increase in vote percentages for incumbents after 1946. Two major problems emerge with accepting the existence of this trend. First, as Garand and Gross (1984) point out, the rise in the vote percentage received by incumbents began in the late 1800s and had virtually ceased by the 1950s. If the rise began that early, and vote percentages essentially ceased to rise after 1950, then the timing of the rise did not coincide with the post-1950 increase in congressional resources that were presumed to provide the means to create personal, nonpartisan, votes.

Second, and more important, however, there are reasons to question whether there was any increase in the vote percentage received by House incumbents after 1950. The much-cited increase in vote percentages was based on analyses of incumbent elections involving only contested incumbents, excluding uncontested seats (Jacobson, 2003b). There were between 80 and 90 uncontested seats in the 1950s and early 1960s, and then the number dropped to between 40 and 60 from 1962 to 1974. As the percentage of uncontested incumbents declined, the previously uncontested seats were added to the average for contested seats. These newly added seats were initially not very competitive, so adding them meant adding in seats with relatively high vote percentages, which raised the overall average vote proportion. If all House elections involving incumbents are included in an analysis covering 1946 to 2000, the percentage of the vote won by incumbents shows no increase over time (Stonecash, 2003a). Figure 1.5 indicates the trend in vote percentages for contested incumbents and for all incumbents from 1946 to 2000. A rise exists only for contested races, but not for all races. If the focus is on the competitiveness of House elections involving incumbents, all

Figure 1.5   Vote Percentages for All Incumbents and for Only Contested Incumbents, 1946–2000

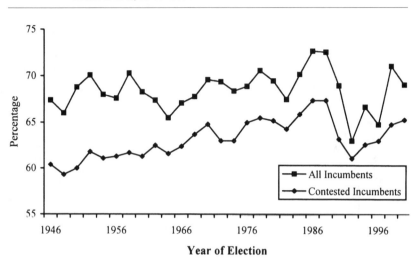

Year of Election

Source: Data compiled by author (see Appendix B).
Note: The vote percentage is the actual percentage of the total vote in a district, not the percentage of the two-party vote.

seats should be included. When they are included, the evidence indicates no increase in the vote proportion of incumbents (Stonecash, 2003b).

Other evidence cited to support the argument that incumbents are "safer" and able to reduce partisan voting also suggests a need to reconsider conventional arguments. A "safe seat" is defined as one in which the candidate won with more than 60 percent of the vote. Beginning in 1966, the percentage of House members with safe seats increased significantly (Mayhew, 1974a; Fiorina, 1977), and that shift persisted in subsequent years (Jacobson, 2001: 27). This shift was taken as evidence that incumbents are able to build personal visibility and electoral loyalties and to increase their vote percentage and diminish competition. The issue is what the 1966 shift really reflects.

If incumbents in general were improving their situation, all incumbents should have been affected. Figure 1.6 presents the percentage of incumbents who received more than 60 percent of the vote, separated by the party of the incumbent. Prior analyses examined all incumbents together. The post-1964 increase in safe seats for all incumbents is

**Figure 1.6   Percentage of House Republican and Democratic Incumbents
Winning with 60 Percent or More of the Vote, 1946–2000**

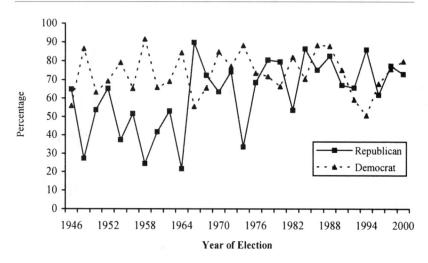

Source: Data compiled by author (see Appendix B).
Note: The vote percentage is the actual percentage of the total vote in a district. This presents all incumbents, contested and uncontested.

almost entirely due to a change in Republican electoral fortunes. From 1946 through 1964, Republican incumbents had fewer safe seats than Democrats. On average, 43.6 percent of Republican incumbent seats were safe, whereas 72.5 percent of Democratic incumbent seats were safe. In 1966, the percentage of safe Republican incumbent seats increased to 89, and averaged 71.3 for the period 1966–2000. Democratic House members experienced little change in the percentage of safe seats, averaging 72.5 for 1946–1964 and 73.2 for 1966–2000. Republicans had more safe seats after 1964, but Democrats did not. The 1966 change, however, cannot reflect a general decline in partisanship and a general "incumbency effect" if the change affects incumbents of only one party.

In sum, two of the central trends that created a perceived need to explain declining partisanship do not indicate that incumbents were increasing their vote percentages, and presumably reducing the role of partisan voting. The vote percentages of all House incumbents did not increase, and the development of a general increase in the "incumbency effect" is in need of reconsideration.[3]

Finally, the fundamental and most serious problem with the view that partisan attachments were declining and that candidate-centered politics were on the rise is that it was accepted without serious consideration of alternative explanations. That is, it was presumed to be a valid explanation of observed changes without considering whether the trends might be explained by other factors. The goal of this analysis is to propose an alternative explanation of why partisanship declined and then returned within the electorate.

The Issue to Be Explained

It was plausible during the 1970s and much of the 1980s to conclude that partisanship within the electorate was declining and that the trend would continue. There was a logical explanation and the data supported the interpretation. Nevertheless, partisan attachments and voting are now on the rise. Something is changing that has been, and is, broadly affecting the extent of partisanship in US politics. It is becoming less plausible to portray US politics as candidate-centered with candidates creating personal electoral images and bases when partisan identification is increasing, partisan voting is increasing, and presidential and House results are increasingly similar across House districts. If House candidates are able to create personal electoral bases that are different from those of presidential candidates, it is unlikely that we would end up with individual partisan behavior driven by the same electoral traits. We need another framework to explain why partisanship declined decades ago and is now returning.

This involves explaining not just current trends, but those that occurred from the 1950s through the 1980s. Was the decline in partisanship that began in the 1960s just a deviation from normalcy, due perhaps to a brief period of political turmoil, and is the current trend a restoration of the norm? Or did something more fundamental change during those years that both led to the appearance of declining partisanship and created the basis for a resurgence of partisanship? Understanding what caused the current situation also has implications for what is likely to occur in the future. If we can understand what created the apparent decline in partisan attachments and then what created their return, we may be able to anticipate whether the current rise will continue.

The Central Argument: Party Realignment
and Its Consequences for Partisanship

The argument of this book is that the parties have undergone long-term secular realignments, and that that process prompted electoral reactions that created the impression that partisanship was declining in importance. In the decades prior to the 1960s, each party coalition contained groups and regions that were in conflict internally but were willing to tolerate each other. The tensions among groups eventually led to conflicts that prompted realignment, with regions and groups gradually shifting their partisan loyalties. This gradual "re-sorting" of the electoral coalitions of each party realigned the electoral bases of the parties, and created the current polarization.[4] As this transition in party electoral bases evolved, it created an era (the 1960s and 1970s) when the composition of each party, as well as the party images, became more diverse. Partisanship declined during this era, and the change was interpreted as the beginning of a decline in parties and partisan attachments.

In fact, that era was one of transition and the beginning of a process that created parties with diverging electoral bases and renewed partisanship. The result is our current resurgent partisanship and polarization. The renewed partisanship of recent years, however, is not simply a restoration of our prior partisanship. Levels of partisanship may have returned to those of prior years, but the basis of the partisanship is now different. A brief summary of the transitions the parties have experienced is presented here. An elaboration of the argument and supporting evidence is presented in subsequent chapters.

The story of change can begin in 1900. The parties in 1900 were heavily regionally based, and these geographical bases resulted in parties with very different policy concerns. The North was developing economically and was largely accepting capitalism and its accompanying changes, as difficult as adjusting to those changes might have been for many workers (Brady, 1988; Sanders, 1999; Bensel, 2000). The South and West were uneasy with capitalism, corporations, and a changing society (Wiebe, 1967; Sanders, 1999). The Republican Party drew almost all of its support from outside the South, whereas the Democratic Party's base was primarily Southern and rural. The Republican Party defended change and its benefits, and the Democratic Party sought to protect farmers and workers who did not fare well as change occurred.

In subsequent decades, the policy concerns of the parties—defending capitalism and change versus trying to help those struggling with capitalism and its effects—had considerable continuity. However, their electoral bases—what areas and what specific groups they represented—began to change. The process of creating change began with the Democratic Party. At least since the 1870s, the Democratic Party had sought to broaden its appeal to urban workers who might need protection from the uncertainties of working conditions within capitalism (Sanders, 1999; James, 2000). Those efforts were met with erratic success through the first two decades of the twentieth century.

During the 1920s and 1930s, changes developed that began the lengthy process of restructuring party electoral bases. Al Smith, New York's Catholic governor from New York City, ran as the Democratic Party's nominee in 1928. He significantly increased Democratic success in Northern urban areas, creating more of an urban base within the party (Degler, 1964; Eldersveld, 1949) but hurting its success in the South. The Great Depression, and the Republican Party's unresponsiveness to the economic crisis, mobilized many new urban voters into the Democratic Party (Andersen, 1979) and increased the party's general level of support outside the South (Sundquist, 1983: 214–228). By the early 1930s, the Democratic Party was faring as well in districts that were more urban, blue collar, Catholic, and industrial as it did in areas that were low on these traits (Brady, 1988: 102). Thus, the Democratic Party in the 1940s and 1950s had a more diverse electoral base and experienced an ongoing tension between a Southern conservative wing and a Northern urban, immigrant, more liberal wing (Reiter, 2001). The Republican Party, based almost exclusively outside the South, continued as an uneasy coalition of liberals, moderates, and conservatives.

The diversity within each party began to increase in the 1960s, creating more intraparty conflict about policy agendas. That internal diversity also reduced the clarity of the policy image of each party. The Democratic Party was generally seen as the more liberal party, but its most prominent spokespersons were often Southern Democrats who were very uneasy about supporting a greater role for government, particularly if it meant federal actions to secure civil rights for blacks. Republicans, some of whom who were willing to support government action to ensure civil rights, were not supportive of higher taxes, more social programs, and more government regulation of business. Conservatives within each party often found themselves having more in common with conservatives from the other party than with some of their own party members. On many issues, the influential coalitions in

Congress were cross-party alliances among conservatives from both parties united against liberals from both parties (*Congressional Quarterly*, 1957–1965).

The resolution of these within-party tensions began to unfold in the 1960s. The Democratic Party had gradually acquired a more urban base from the 1930s through the 1960s (Turner and Schneier, 1970: 118). Beginning in 1964, the Democrats enacted a large body of legislation expanding existing government social programs and adding new programs in a wide array of areas. Welfare rights were increased; government-enforced civil rights were established in voting, employment, and housing; education aid was increased; and medical care programs for the elderly and the poor were established.

The outburst of legislation created many unhappy conservatives within the Democratic Party. The expansion of the role of government through all these programs also left many conservative Republicans unhappy, and they began the process of appealing to Democratic conservatives to bring them to the Republican Party (Brennan, 1995; Hodgson, 1996). The Republican Party began a gradual and contentious shift to a more conservative stance. By the late 1980s, with its consistent opposition to taxes and government, the Republican Party began to be seen as the clearly more conservative party. The party attracted more of a white, affluent base that was opposed to an activist government unless it was to encourage cultural values through legislation and regulation. Republicans mobilized more conservatives into the Republican Party (Stonecash, 2000: 65), particularly within the South (Black and Black, 1987, 2002).

The movement of conservatives out of the Democratic Party, the enfranchisement of blacks, the steady immigration of Hispanics, and electoral alignments revolving around race (Carmines and Stimson, 1989), class (Stonecash, 2000), religion (Layman, 2001), and ideology (Abramowitz, 1994; Abramowitz and Saunders, 1998) created a Democratic Party with a clearer liberal image. This gradual realignment of both parties, which was given less attention by academics concerned with finding abrupt, critical realignments (Shafer, 1991), has created parties with diverging electoral bases and images.

The long-term changes in the parties' electoral bases have had three important consequences for partisanship. First, as the parties experienced transitions in their electoral bases during the 1960s and 1970s, the clarity of each party's image about policy positions diminished. Democrats maintained their Southern base during the 1950s and 1960s while acquiring a more urban, non-Southern electoral base, reducing the clarity of the policy image. At the same time, the Republican Party experienced ongoing struggles over whether it should be libertarian and support capitalism and free markets or emphasize using government to enforce the goals of social conservatives (Dionne, 1997: 199–299). Within each party, there was considerable dispute about what direction the party should take as well as uncertainty about whether seeking to attract particular constituencies was likely to succeed. Republicans, for example, argued over whether issues such as opposition to affirmative action should be emphasized, and whether it was really possible to attract Southern whites after a century of their strong attachment to the Democratic Party. Voters might well have been uncertain about the likely future direction of each party. Election results added to the uncertainty. A party would make inroads into particular areas in one election and then lose some of those seats in subsequent elections, leading to doubts about whether change was actually proceeding in a particular direction.

In addition, the public image of each party was clouded by incumbents who survived as electoral bases were shifting and whose public pronouncements, alongside those of newer members, diminished the clarity of party images. Congressional Democrats in the 1970s, for example, had liberal, Northern members and longstanding incumbents from the South who were very conservative. This combination, of course, created some ambiguity about the party's image. As each party struggled to negotiate internal conflicts among its factions and to decide what policy directions it would emphasize, the clarity of concern before the electorate undoubtedly declined. That, in turn, may have led to many voters seeing less of a difference between the parties, resulting in diminished partisan attachments.

Second, these intraparty struggles, as they evolved, resulted in secular realignment. Many conservatives moved out of the Democratic Party to the Republican Party, and more liberals moved to the Democratic Party (Abramowitz and Saunders, 1998). This process reduced the internal diversity of each party and created parties with electoral bases that are now very different from each other (Fleisher and Bond, 2000: 166; (Stonecash et al., 2002) and even more polarized (Grosclose et al., 1999). Thus, the renewed partisanship we are witnessing now is a reflection of this gradual realignment and the greater differences in the party bases.

Third, these changes developed slowly, and we should expect the electorate to perceive and react to these changes just as slowly (Popkin,

1994). The transition of the Democratic Party to being more urban and liberal began in the 1920s, but its identity as being more of an urban party evolved over decades. Not until the 1980s did the party really begin to lose its Southern, rural, conservative wing and acquire a clear identity among voters as the urban, liberal alternative. The Republican Party also evolved slowly. It has never been a liberal party, but for much of the century it held many seats in Congress in the more liberal North, resulting in a party containing many moderates. That changed, beginning in the 1960s, when the party began to adopt more conservative positions and gradually win seats in the South and attract conservatives (Black and Black, 2002: 328–368).

As the positions of the parties continued to evolve during the 1980s and 1990s, many voters began to change their partisanship. Two groups are particularly important in this respect. First, some of those who had seen little difference between the parties during the transition era and who identified themselves as independent began to identify with a party. Their alignments created greater partisanship. Second, those who had faced a conflict between their own policy preferences and those of "their" party began to move to the other major party. The net result was an increase in the percentage of the electorate identifying with a party, and those voters who identified with a party were also inclined to vote for candidates from that party.

The story, then, is one of gradual transition, with small percentages of voters steadily shifting their party identifications over time. The parties have ultimately remained very central to voters, but the transition process created the impression that a decline in partisan attachments was occurring. The goal of this analysis is to explain the changes in party electoral bases that led to the period of transition and then to the reemergence of strong partisanship.

2

The Great Transition

The electoral bases of the parties have changed enormously in the last century. In 1900, the parties were defined largely by their regional bases of support. This dominance of regionalism has declined, opening the way for cleavages revolving around race, class, ideology, and religion to emerge as more significant. Region has come to matter less and individual traits and beliefs now matter more. These evolutions have created the basis for the renewed party polarization and partisanship evident in the electorate over the last decade or so. The lengthy and gradual overall evolution of these changes is reviewed first in this chapter. The transition that occurred from the 1960s through the 1980s is examined at the end of this chapter.

Regionalism and Its Erosion

Regional divisions were very significant in 1900 and lasted for decades. The South was heavily Democratic in the late 1800s and it became more so around the turn of the century. The remainder of the nation was primarily Republican and it also became more so after 1900. This regional division was driven by different interests and different visions of the ideal society.

Southern farmers, much like farmers in the West, were uneasy about the effects of industrial change, and they disliked their dependence on Northern railroads and bankers (Goodwyn, 1978). The Southern farmers' ideal was agrarian life with its small, self-sustaining communities of highly intertwined people (Wiebe, 1967). They were suspicious of Catholicism, its emphasis on hierarchical authority, and immigrant lifestyles in urban Northern cities. They also wanted to preserve the Southern practice of a strictly racially segregated way of life (Kousser, 1974). Beginning almost immediately after the Southern states were readmitted to the Union and Reconstruction collapsed (Foner, 1988), the South began to steadily become more Democratic. During the late 1800s, the South restricted the suffrage of blacks and low-income whites, and the remaining Southern electorate became heavily Democratic, with very few Republicans winning any seats in the South.

The North, in contrast, was industrializing, and as the 1800s came to an end, there was more support within that region for the Republican vision of accepting change and economic development than embracing the South's negative reaction to industrialization (Bensel, 2000). Following the 1896 clash between Republican William McKinley, who supported industrialization, and Democratic William Jennings Bryan, who espoused the virtues of small-town, agrarian life, the South became even more Democratic, and the rest of the nation became more Republican (Brady, 1988; Stonecash and Silina, 2005).

The Democratic Shift

The result was a significant political division by region. Table 2.1 presents Democratic success in winning votes and in securing House seats and electoral-college votes in 1900 for the South[5] and the non-South. In 1900, Democratic Party House and presidential candidates won a high percentage of the vote in the South, and did much worse outside the South. Perhaps most important, the party's ability to win congressional seats was much greater in the South. In the House, Democratic candidates won 63.9 percent of the vote within the region, and 95.6 percent of all seats within the region. Nationally, 54.1 percent of the party's seats in the House of Representatives came from the South. The Democratic presidential candidate won 61.5 percent of the vote in the South and 100 percent of all electoral votes within the South. In 1900, 63.6 percent of all Democratic electoral votes came from the South. The regional split in 1900 was not atypical of the era. For the presidential elections of 1900 through 1908, the average percentage of the vote won in the South by Democratic presidential candidates was 64.1 percent, and House candidates received an average of 72.8 percent.

Table 2.1 Regionalism in 1900: Democratic Success

	South	Non-South
House elections		
Percentage of seats won	95.6	27.3
Percentage of vote won	63.9	44.5
Percentage of seats from	54.1	45.9
Presidential elections		
Percentage of vote won	61.5	43.0
Percentage of electoral votes won	100.0	12.8
Percentage of electoral votes from	63.6	36.4

Source: Jerrold G. Rusk, *A Statistical History of the American Electorate* (Washington, D.C.: Congressional Quarterly Press, 2001), p. 139 (presidential popular vote), p. 141 (electoral votes), p. 233 (House votes), and p. 260 (seats won).

Outside the South, in that same period, Democratic presidential candidates averaged 39.3 percent and House candidates 40.9 percent of the vote. The Democratic Party was primarily a Southern party, receiving its highest vote percentage in a region that was heavily rural compared to the rest of the nation.

Even though the party was based primarily in the South, a region often identified as conservative due to its discriminatory racial practices, Democrats were not a party just seeking to limit government and preserve segregation practices. In matters other than race, Democrats were pursuing policies to help those struggling to adapt as industrialization and urbanization unfolded. Although the party was primarily Southern, it had some success in the West and it was seeking to expand beyond its base. Voters in both regions of the country were troubled by the power of railroads and banks over their lives. Railroads and shippers, who controlled the availability and cost of storage options before goods were shipped, as well as the cost of shipping, therefore controlled the ability of farmers to ship their products to Eastern markets. Banks had additional influence. They set rates for loans to pay for land and supplies, giving rise to continual accusations that Eastern banks charged higher interest rates for credit to those from the South and West (Bensel, 2000: 264–268). The Democrats from the South and West continually sought to pass legislation, or to strengthen existing relevant laws, that would regulate the practices of railroads (Sanders, 1999: 179–216). Democrats pursued efforts that were liberal in the sense that the party was seeking to use the power of government to address perceived inequities and to regulate the private sector to improve the fortunes of those not doing well.

The Democratic Party knew that if its electoral base was largely confined to the South, it would not be able to win presidential elections. A presidential candidate had to secure at least a plurality in some states outside the South to be able to win the presidency (James, 2000: 1–35). During the late 1800s and the early 1900s, Democratic leaders continually sought to build a coalition comprising farmers in the South and urban workers in the North. Republicans had acquired political dominance around 1900 because urban areas had become more Republican (Degler, 1964). Republicans in the early 1900s did well in urban areas, but their majorities in the large cities were modest, so Democrats thought they could attract greater support in those areas. The Democratic Party regularly proposed legislation that would require better working conditions for industrial workers, in the hope of attracting their votes (Sanders, 1999: 340–386; James, 2000; 123–199). The party also supported pro-Catholic positions, opposing alcohol prohibition laws and supporting parochial schools. The hope was that by indicating support for urban workers and Catholic ethnics, Democrats could pull them away from a Republican Party that supported the changes accompanying capitalism and was fundamentally unsympathetic to the concerns of labor and Catholics. These efforts yielded limited success during the first two decades of the century, and in 1920 the party remained largely a rural party (Burner, 1968: 3–15). Woodrow Wilson had won the presidency by appealing to the South and West, and the party had members who were anti-Catholic and in favor of prohibition, stances that alienated urban immigrants in the North and Northeast.

The first changes in the Democratic Party's electoral base emerged in the 1920s as the party made inroads into urban areas. The party had historically had a rural base, but elements of the party had shown sympathy for the problems that urban immigrants faced in a society that often did not welcome them. Simple pragmatists within the party recognized that the United States was becoming more urban and that any future success would hinge on the ability to gain votes among the growing urban constituency in the country (James, 2000: 1–35). The Democratic Party conventions of 1924 and 1928 reflected these tensions, with urban and rural factions fighting over the direction of the party (Burner, 1968: 74–102). The 1928 nomination of New York Governor Al Smith, a Catholic from New York City, as the party's presidential candidate resulted in significant gains in Northern urban areas, even while Southerners reacted very negatively to his Catholic background.

The 1932 election produced even more significant gains for Democrats in Northern urban areas. The Great Depression had started in 1929, and President Herbert Hoover and the Republicans were reluctant to act in response and thus developed an image of being unwilling to do anything to help the unemployed (Sundquist, 1983: 198–207), resulting in a dramatic shift toward the Democratic Party in 1932 in urban areas (Lubell, 1956). Once Democrats acquired power, they enacted extensive legislation intended to help the economy and the unemployed (Sundquist, 1983: 208–239). These positions mobilized many urban constituents who had previously not participated in politics (Andersen, 1979), and Democrats built on their gains in urban areas in 1932 and further increased their urban vote totals in 1936 (Eldersveld, 1949; Degler, 1964; Clubb and Allen, 1969).

The result was a new Democratic majority, but a majority party that had a different composition than before and had significant internal tensions. Most of the seats added to the Democratic Party came from outside the South. In 1928, 92 of 166 House Democratic seats had come from the South, comprising 55.4 percent of the House party. By 1934, 101 of their 315 seats came from the South, comprising only 32.1 percent of the party. The Democratic Party was now a party with a conservative anti-federal government wing and a more liberal urban, ethnic, labor base (Reiter, 2001). The Northern wing was more inclined to enact social programs and willing to pursue issues of banning lynching in the South, whereas the Southern wing wanted no intrusion into the Southern way of life. Democrats from the South were willing to go along with the enactment of new social programs, such as a national welfare program, only if they were enacted with provisions allowing significant state autonomy to limit benefits and determine who was eligible (Derthick, 1970; Mettler, 1998).

Although the wings struggled to reach agreements over the way social programs should be structured (Derthick, 1970; Mettler, 1998), race was a particularly divisive issue. Northerners wanted to stop lynching in the South, but could not muster enough votes to pass legislation (Turner and Schneier, 1970: 137–143). Race issues emerged as particularly significant during the 1948 presidential election. President Truman took a series of steps in 1947 and 1948 that alienated the South, and the region was never as solidly Democratic again. In December 1946, Truman established, via executive order, a Civil Rights Committee to study conditions within the United States (Gardner, 2002: 14–15). In June 1947, Truman became the first president to accept an offer to speak before the National Association for the Advancement of Colored People (NAACP), where he forcefully supported equal rights for blacks (pp. 28–29). When his Civil Rights Committee submitted a report detailing unequal treatment and suggesting a federal role in remedying the problem, he publicly embraced it (pp. 43–64). He made civil rights central to his 1948 State of the Union address, and later that year he submitted legislation to Congress to implement the recommendations of his committee (pp. 65–86). He supported a strong civil rights plank in the Democratic Party's convention of 1948 and issued executive orders desegregating the federal workforce and the armed services (pp. 87–111).

In response to these efforts to change racial segregation practices in the South, the Dixiecrat Party formed and nominated Democratic segregationist Strom Thurmond as its presidential candidate. Thurmond took large portions of the vote away from Truman and permanently lowered the Democratic presidential vote in the South. The impact of the 1948 election in the South is shown in Figure 2.1. It presents the percentage of the vote received by Democratic and Republican candidates from 1904 to 1964 in the South. From 1904 to 1944, except for 1928, Democratic candidates received 65–80 percent of the vote within the

Figure 2.1   Support for Presidential Candidates in the South, 1904–1964

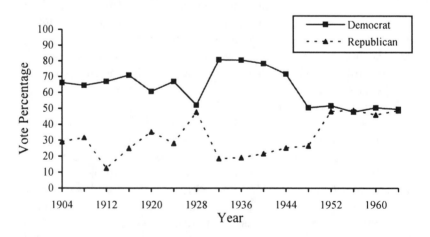

Source: Jerrold G. Rusk, *A Statistical History of the American Electorate* (Washington, D.C.: Congressional Quarterly Press, 2001), pp. 139–140.

South. In 1948, that percentage dropped to 51.8, with 23.0 percent of the vote going to Thurmond. The Democratic percentage of the vote never returned to its former levels. The percentage that had gone to Thurmond moved to the Republican Party and stayed there. The South had begun to move to the Republican Party. Republicans realized continued success in 1952 and 1956 when they ran Dwight Eisenhower, a respected war leader, as their candidate. He attracted almost 50 percent of the vote in the South, and contributed to the conviction that Republicans could make inroads into the South.

The consequence of the 1948 shift was disruption of a longstanding regional partisan division in American politics. The distribution of partisan support across the states that existed in 1900 had continued up until the 1948 election with little disruption. States that voted heavily Democratic in 1900 voted heavily Democratic in subsequent years. Figure 2.2 indicates this stability and 1948's disruption of it. In this analysis, the focus is on votes for Democratic presidential and House candidates by state.[6] The concern is whether the degree of partisan support within a state in successive elections from 1904 to 1960 was reflec-

Figure 2.2   Correlation of Presidential and House Votes, by State, for 1904–1960 with 1900 Results

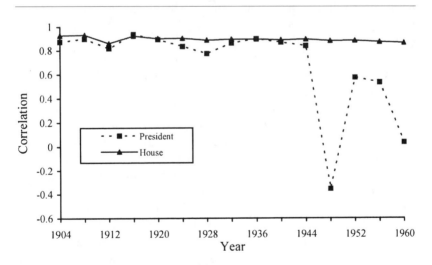

Source: State level voting results presented in Jerrold G. Rusk, *A Statistical History of the American Electorate* (Washington, D.C.: Congressional Quarterly Press, 2001), Tables 4-24 to 4-36 for years 1900 to 1996.

tive of the 1900 level of support. Did states that were strongly Democratic in 1900 stay that way, and did states that weakly supported Democrats stay that way?

To assess this, the percentages by state of those supporting Democratic presidential and House candidates for each office for 1904 through 1960 are correlated with partisan percentages in 1900 (Paulson, 2000: 23–34).[7] If states are stable in their relative positions, the correlation should be high. The correlation of results from 1904 to 1944 with those of 1900 for both offices is about 0.9. Then the correlation of 1948 presidential results with the 1900 presidential percentages plummeted. Although this correlation came back somewhat in 1952 and 1956, it never again approached the 1904–1944 levels. In 1960, presidential results had no association with results from 1900, indicating significant change was under way. House results remained very stable during this time, as the South remained staunchly Democratic in congressional elections. Nonetheless, the disruption of the 1900–1944 stability of Democratic presidential support was a sign that partisan change was possible in the South.

The elections of 1948 and the 1950s gave Republicans hope, and the actions of Democrats in the mid-1960s provided Republicans with greater opportunities to make further inroads into the South. President Lyndon Johnson pushed Congress to enact several civil rights laws and numerous social programs that bestowed significant benefits on minorities. At the same time, Republican presidential candidate Barry Goldwater opposed the 1964 Civil Rights Act. For the first time in a century, the Republican Party was identified with opposition to civil rights for blacks, and non-Southern Democrats supported the new laws. This legislation produced a significant increase in black registration (Stonecash et al., 2003: 55) and a shift in black support away from the Republican Party and to the Democratic Party (Carmines and Stimson, 1989).[8] These events also prompted many white Southerners to give more consideration to the Republican Party.

The rise in black registration and growing differences between the parties on issues of race and social programs were creating a long-term transition of the South away from the Democratic Party (Black and Black, 1987; 2002). The changes were by no means abrupt and uniform across offices. Democratic presidential candidates experienced erosion in electoral support in the South before congressional candidates did. Figure 2.3 indicates the vote percentage for Democratic House and presidential candidates in the South throughout the last century. House

**Figure 2.3   Overall Vote Percentage Within the South, Democratic
House and Presidential Candidates, 1900–2000**

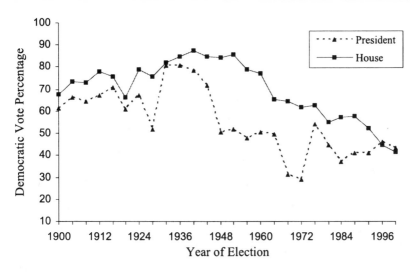

Source: Regional voting results presented in Jerrold G. Rusk, *A Statistical History of the American Electorate* (Washington, D.C.: Congressional Quarterly Press, 2001), Table 5-8.

incumbents were able to hold off the encroachment of Republican success for decades. Whereas Democratic presidential success declined abruptly in 1948, the decline for Southern Democratic House candidates was much more gradual. Indeed, it was not until the 1996 election that the overall vote percentages for House and presidential candidates in the South again converged. The last year that that had occurred was 1932. Changes in partisan support in the South were lengthy but steady in evolving.

The 1932 election brought the Democratic Party a Northern, urban, and more liberal constituency that would ultimately prompt a decline in its support within the South. The more immediate effect of the 1932 election, however, was an improvement of its fortunes outside the South. As Figure 2.4 indicates, in the early 1900s, Democratic presidential and House candidates were receiving roughly 40 percent of their overall vote from outside the South. The 1932 election boosted their percentage to over 50, and, despite some fluctuations in later years, the party was able to sustain its relative success outside the South through the rest of the century, even while the South was shifting away from the

Figure 2.4   Overall Democratic Percentage of the Vote Outside the South, Presidential and House Candidates, 1900–2000

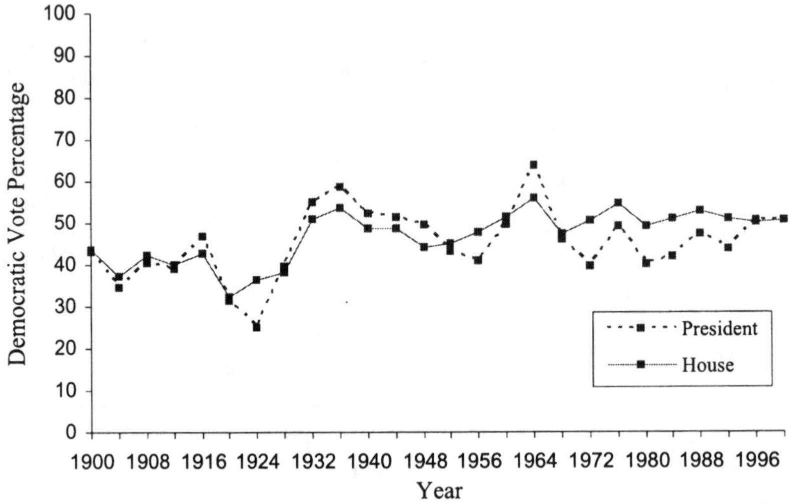

Source: Derived from regional voting results presented in Jerrold G. Rusk, *A Statistical History of the American Electorate* (Washington, D.C.: Congressional Quarterly Press, 2001), Table 5-8.

party. The 1932 election, then, was the beginning of a major shift in American politics. The full impact of that election took decades to unfold, but it eventually prompted significant change.

The Republican Shift

The Republican Party also experienced changes as the century evolved, but they developed later and more gradually than for the Democratic Party. There was no major shift until 1994 that affected the party's situation. From the 1870s through the 1950s, the Republican Party won virtually no seats in the South while winning 60 percent or more of all House elections outside the South. The party was heavily reliant on areas outside the South until 1960.

But even though Republicans dominated areas outside the South, the party was not without its own internal tensions, and these tensions also eventually resulted in change. The issue that proved to be crucial was how much government should intrude in the private sector and the larger society. The dominant wing of the party, largely based in the East and Midwest, was not completely hostile to having government play a role in society. Congressional members from these areas were willing to consider civil rights legislation and would support modest social programs. The Western wing of the party, in contrast, was much more hostile to taxes, regulations, and social programs and was more likely to embrace libertarian notions that individual freedom was more important than government assistance (Rae, 1989: 29–43; Brennan, 1995: 5–7).

The tension between the two wings became more serious during the 1950s and 1960s. The 1958 elections resulted in significant Republican losses, with many Northern Republicans, liberal on race issues, losing to liberal Northern Democrats (Carmines and Stimson, 1989: 69–72). That election reduced the dominance of the Eastern liberal wing within the party. Just as important, during the 1950s and the early 1960s, the antigovernment conservatives began to mobilize other conservatives to oppose the programs of the New Deal and a greater federal role in society. These conservatives stressed their faith in individualism, free enterprise, and less government (Rae, 1989: 48–52; Brennan, 1995: 8).

The more conservative Republicans found a voice in Barry Goldwater in the 1960s. Goldwater, frustrated with Eisenhower's acceptance of the New Deal, had emerged as a leader of the conservative wing of the party in the late 1950s. He eventually secured the 1964 Republican nomination for president, but lost in a landslide. Democrats gained enough seats to enable them to enact new federal programs such as Medicaid and Medicare in 1965–1968. This burst of liberal legislation convinced many conservative Republicans that they needed to mobilize to oppose the growth of government in US society. They saw a greater federal government as more intrusive and as detrimental to preserving freedom in US society. Conservatives whom Goldwater had recruited for the 1964 campaign remained in many party positions following the election, and they worked to recruit and elect more conservatives. Even though many moderates and liberals within the party thought the 1964 loss consigned conservatives to insignificance, conservatives renewed their efforts to organize so they could advocate their views (Perlstein, 2001; Edwards, 1999).

Much as Democratic presidential candidates had sought votes in the North in the early 1900s to expand their base, Republican presidential candidates saw the potential of seeking votes in the South to improve their chances of winning presidential elections and a majority in Congress. Nixon pursued a "Southern Strategy" in 1968 and 1972, seeking to take votes away from George Wallace (Carter, 1995: 324–414). He did so by seeking to reassure white Southerners that he would not be too aggressive in pushing integration. There was considerable ambiguity in Nixon's positions, however. His presidency presented mixed signals, as he established the Environmental Protection Agency (EPA), proposed a guaranteed income for the poor, sought programs to increase minority employment on construction projects, but also opposed busing and efforts to help minorities.

Conservatives continued to push their argument that the role of government should be limited. They wanted the Republican Party to serve as the vehicle for challenging the growing role of the national government in US society. New think tanks funded by wealthy conservatives emerged to support research and essays by conservatives (Ricci, 1993; Stefancic and Delgado, 1997; Covington, 1998). These critics argued that many government programs did more harm than good because they discouraged responsibility and adaptation to private markets. Indeed, by the early 1980s, conservatives were arguing that government actions in the area of welfare, despite good intentions, were making things worse (Murray, 1984; Magnet, 1993; Hodgson, 1996: 130–139).

The exception to a diminished role for government involved issues of personal morality. Many conservatives argued that liberals had created a permissive environment that was leading to more prolonged stays on welfare as well as more crime, divorce, abortions, and illegitimate births. They saw government-imposed rules (for example, those banning abortion, imposing tougher penalties for crime, and limiting welfare) as a way to alter morality patterns, and they saw the Republican Party as the vehicle to enact these changes (Green et al., 1998). Conservatives were able to present a vision of government as intrusive and oppressive while also presenting it as a vehicle to remedy problems of morality in society (Dionne, 1997: 199–299).

By the late 1970s, the Republican Party was a coalition of Northern moderate Republicans (fiscally conservative but moderate on civil liberties, civil rights, and social issues) and Southern and Western conservatives, who were much more hostile to government intrusion except on issues of morality. Over time, the former part of this coalition has declined and the latter group of conservatives has come to dominate the party. The party made steady inroads into the South and the Sun Belt, and conservatives continued to organize to acquire more power within the party. They sought tax cuts, were opposed to a significant role for the federal government, and supported a conservative social agenda. The election of Ronald Reagan was an indicator that antigovernment conservatives were gaining influence within the party. Reagan thought government was too big and too intrusive, and he took too much of people's money. He wanted to cut back on federal welfare, and he endorsed the idea that welfare created dependency, so government should cut welfare and return people to independence. He wanted less government in the broad area of social programs, but a stronger defense (Palmer and Sawhill, 1982, 1984).

This shift in policy emphasis within the party attracted even more conservatives. From the early 1970s to the mid-1980s, conservative whites who were opposed to government efforts to guarantee jobs, as well as easy access to abortion, steadily moved to the Republican Party (Carmines and Stanley, 1990: 28–29). In the South, conservatives and the affluent were steadily leaving the Democratic Party and moving to the Republican Party (Black and Black, 1987: 249–254; Brewer and Stonecash, 2001). The transition of the Republican Party from being moderate-conservative and Northern to being a primarily conservative party with growing contingents from the South and the Sun Belt was evolving slowly with antigovernment conservatives steadily becoming a greater part of the party.

In summary, each party has experienced lengthy and significant changes in its electoral base. The Democratic Party has acquired more of an urban, nonwhite, and non-Southern constituency. The gradual loss of conservative Southerners during the 1960s and 1970s resulted in a Democratic Party with a diverse constituency and a murky image. Conversely, the Republican Party has acquired an electoral base that is more conservative and antigovernment, but this transition has also been gradual, resulting in a diverse party throughout the 1970s and into the 1990s.

3

The Consequences of Change

The lengthy realignment experienced by each party created a series of changes that resulted first in a decline and then in a resurgence of partisan attachments within the electorate in the 1990s and after. The first and most obvious change was that realignment created a steady erosion of the regionalism that had dominated US politics for decades. This decline of regional attachments opened the door for other bases of conflict to emerge. As Key (1949: 315–316) argued long ago in assessing the South, when one region sees itself as pitted against another, it creates unity within the region and suppresses other conflicts that might divide people within the region. The decline of regionalism made it possible for the parties to attract constituencies that had previously based their partisan allegiances primarily on regional loyalties. The emergence of these new party electoral bases eventually created more clarity of the electoral bases and images of the parties, and explains the reemergence of strong partisanship in the electorate in the last decade or so.

These changes, however, did not unfold rapidly, and it was often difficult to be sure what evolutions were occurring and were likely to continue to occur. The transition in the bases and images of the parties, in the 1960s and 1970s increased the presence of independents and ticket-splitting in the short run. With the party electoral bases shifting, the parties became more internally diverse and less different from each other. For many voters, there was less urgency in being a Democrat or Republican. For others holding specific public policy views, the transitions of the parties created a sense that they were in the wrong party, and that they should leave their party.

This chapter reviews data about these trends. The subsequent chapters apply this framework to explaining trends in three central indicators of partisanship: the rise and decline of split outcomes in House districts, ticket-splitting, and independents.

The Erosion of Regionalism

The change in the role of regionalism and in the regional bases of the parties has been dramatic. The Democratic Party in the early 1900s won almost all House seats in the South. As shown in Figure 3.1, Democrats consistently won at least 90 percent of seats in House elections in the South from 1900 until the 1960s. Although the Democrats completely dominated Southern contests in those years, they struggled to win seats elsewhere. Outside the South, Democrats experienced success in 1912, when the Progressive Party disrupted Republicans, and again in 1932 to 1940, but they did not reach sustained success outside the South until 1958. The result was that the Democratic Party in the House relied

Figure 3.1   Percentage of US House Seats Won by Democrats, by Region, 1900–2002

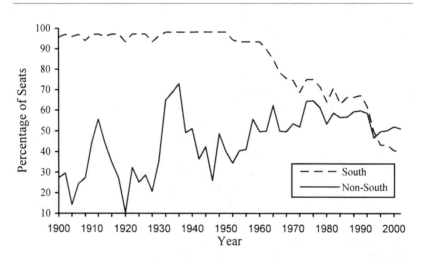

Sources: Regional voting results presented in Jerrold G. Rusk, *A Statistical History of the American Electorate* (Washington, D.C.: Congressional Quarterly Press, 2001), Table 5-8. Data compiled by the author.

heavily on Southern seats until well into the 1950s. By the 1970s, the party was experiencing equal success in the South and outside the South. A remarkable regional division that had begun in the late 1800s had taken until the 1970s to erode.

As this pronounced regional split eroded, the Democratic Party's heavy reliance on the South also steadily diminished. As Figure 3.2 indicates, as late as the 1950s the party was consistently deriving at least 40 percent of its House seats from the South. An exception occurred in the 1930s, when the party did not lose Southern seats, and even gained seats outside the South. The transition in the party's base in the latter half of the twentieth century steadily decreased the importance of Southern seats, even as the South was growing as a percentage of the nation's population.

The same transition occurred for presidential candidates, for whom the crucial matter is winning electoral college votes. The electoral college, with minor exceptions, is a winner-take-all system within states,[9] or all votes from a state go to the candidate with a plurality. This rule leads to exaggerated influence of regions because a candidate need win

Figure 3.2   Percentage of Democratic House Seats Derived from Regions, 1900–2002

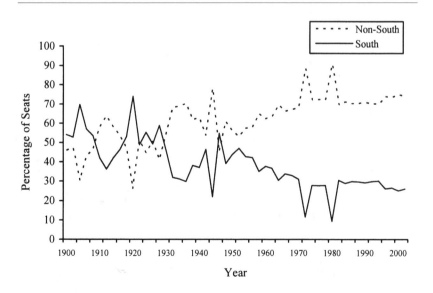

Source: Data compiled by the author.

only a plurality of the vote in states within a region. With that caution in mind, the results over time for Democratic candidates are revealing of the change experienced by the party. Figure 3.3 presents the percentages of all Democratic presidential electoral college votes derived from the South and the remainder of the nation from 1900 to 2000.

In the early 1900s, the Democratic Party derived most of its electoral college votes from the South. Franklin Roosevelt was able to broaden the party's appeal, and for the 1932 through 1948 elections, the South was less dominant as a percentage of the Democratic presidential electoral base. The success of Republican Dwight Eisenhower outside the South pushed Democrats back to their Southern base in 1952 and 1956. Beginning with the 1960 campaign, however, the party reduced its reliance on the South, and with the exception of a run by Georgia

Figure 3.3   Democratic Source of Electoral College Votes, South and Non-South, 1900–2000

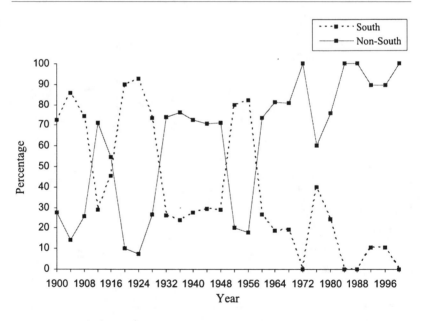

Sources: Results presented in Jerrold G. Rusk, *A Statistical History of the American Electorate* (Washington, D.C.: Congressional Quarterly Press, 2001), Table 4-3. Data compiled by the author.

Governor Jimmy Carter in 1976, reliance on the South diminished steadily after that. Even Bill Clinton, a former governor of Arkansas, did not derive a significant percentage of his electoral votes from the South in 1992 and 1996.

Republicans, of course, were experiencing the opposite changes. As Figure 3.4 indicates, from 1900 through 1960, almost all Republican House seats came from outside the South. As of 1960, the party seemed very limited in its ability to broaden its base into the South.

Presidential elections became the means by which the Republican Party began to change its success in the South. In 1952 and 1956, Republican presidential candidate Dwight Eisenhower, won almost 50 percent of the vote in the South (Figure 3.5). In the 1964 election, Republican presidential candidate Barry Goldwater won a higher per-centage in the South than outside the South—the first time that that occurred in the twentieth century. Through the next 30 years, the party generally did somewhat better in the South than outside the South.

Figure 3.4   Percentage of Republican Seats from Each Region, US House, 1900–2002

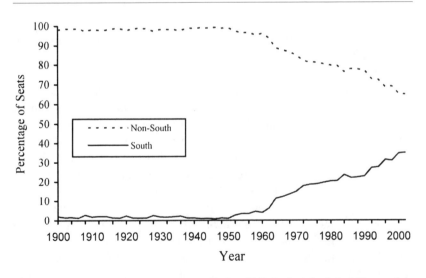

Sources: Regional voting results presented in Jerrold G. Rusk, *A Statistical History of the American Electorate* (Washington, D.C.: Congressional Quarterly Press, 2001), Table 5-8, and data compiled by the author.

**Figure 3.5   Percentage of Votes Won by Republican Presidential Candidates,
South and Non-South, 1900–2000**

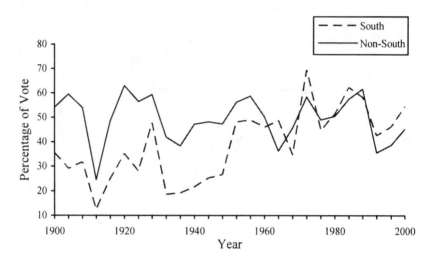

Sources: Regional voting results presented in Jerrold G. Rusk, *A Statistical History of the
American Electorate* (Washington, D.C.: Congressional Quarterly Press, 2001). Table 5-8, and
data compiled by the author.

Since 1992, the relative success of Republican presidential candidates
in the South has been more consistent, at 7–9 percentage points better in
the South than outside the South.

These trends have altered the Republicans' source of electoral
votes. Figure 3.6 indicates the changes that Republican presidential
candidates have experienced. From 1900 through 1948, Republicans
almost always derived 100 percent of their electoral college votes from
non-Southern states. That began to change in 1952, however, and after
some delay the South steadily became more important to the party
beginning in 1980. From 1992 to 2000, more than 50 percent of the
Republican electoral college votes came from the South. Some of this
change, of course, reflects the growing percentage of the US public living in the South, but the primary source of change is the increasing success of Republicans in the South (Black and Black, 1992, 2002).

These transitions all reflect the demise of the regional division of
the late 1800s and early 1900s. The extent of the shift can be seen by
comparing partisan support for presidential candidates from 1900 by

Figure 3.6   Republican Source of Electoral Votes, South and Non-South, 1900–2000

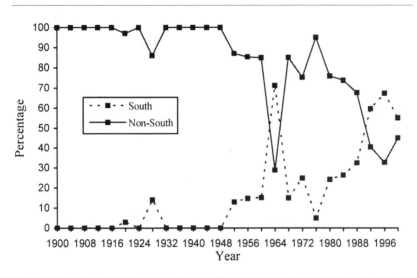

Sources: Results presented in Jerrold G. Rusk, *A Statistical History of the American Electorate* (Washington, D.C.: Congressional Quarterly Press, 2001). Table 4-3, and data compiled by the author.

state with subsequent support levels, as was done in Chapter 2. Figure 3.7 extends the analysis presented in Figure 2.2 through the 2002 elections. Again, Democratic vote percentages for state-level results from the years after 1900 are correlated with percentages for 1900 for House and presidential contests. If a state's relative degree of support for a party's candidates is stable over time, the correlation will remain high. The trend of the correlation indicates steady change over time in the relative positions of states (Paulson, 2000: 23–34). The correlation of 1904 with 1900 is 0.87. The correlation of later years (1904, 1908, 1912, and later) with 1900 slides gradually to around 0 in 1960 and then becomes somewhat negative, with the 2000 correlation with 1900 at –0.26. House results, aggregated to the state level, follow the same pattern of change, but with considerable delay. Thus, over the course of 100 years, the prior regional party dominance disappeared, and Republicans now do somewhat better where Democrats once dominated. There is now some reversal of the prior regional loyalties, but that has not produced the simple, clear regional division that prevailed in 1900.

Figure 3.7   Correlation of Presidential and House Votes, by State, for 1904–2002 with 1900 Results

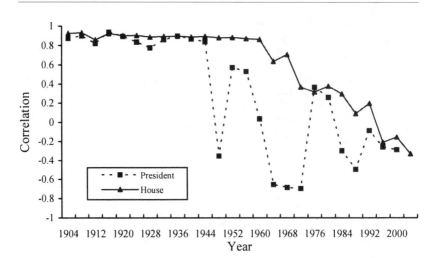

Sources: State level voting results presented in Jerrold G. Rusk, *A Statistical History of the American Electorate* (Washington, D.C.: Congressional Quarterly Press, 2001). Tables 4-24 through 4-36 for years 1900–1996. Results from The Federal Election Commission website for 2000 and 2002.

The Emergence of New Bases of Political Divisions: Aggregate Evidence

The decline of the regional attachments of 1900 created the possibility for other political divisions to emerge. The Democratic Party up until the 1930s was primarily concerned with creating government rules to protect those being hurt by economic change. The party was not, however, supportive of the modern welfare state with its many programs that provide assistance to the elderly, the poor, those attending college, local school districts, and cities. Republicans were concerned with constraining government intrusion into business activities, but were willing to use government to support the creation of the infrastructure of transportation and communications that helped to promote economic development.

In retrospect, the Great Depression was a crucial stimulus for change for the parties. With high and sustained long-term unemployment following the stock market crash of 1929, the issue was how the parties would respond. Whereas Democrats were ambivalent about just how to respond between 1929 and 1932, Republicans were adamant that nothing should be done, believing the problem would correct itself (Schlesinger, 1957). The electorate largely rejected the Republican approach, and Roosevelt found himself with a substantially different electoral base than the Democratic Party previously had. The candidacy of Al Smith (Democratic governor from New York) in 1928 had increased Democratic success in urban areas (Degler, 1964). The Great Depression and Hoover's unwillingness to respond generated even more Democratic votes in the large cities (Eldersveld, 1949; Lubell, 1956; Turner and Schneier, 1970: 118; Andersen, 1979). Democrats, realizing they had improved their success in urban areas for two consecutive elections, recognized that they had to do something for the urban unemployed if they were to hold that constituency (Sundquist, 1983: 198–214). The result was that Democrats in the 1930s were willing to sponsor legislation to provide job protections, encourage unions, and create jobs at a time when the economy was slow to respond. Although Democrats lost some of their support in urban areas after 1932 and 1936, they did not drop back to the levels they experienced prior to 1928.

Of interest is how the relationship of the Democratic vote to urban areas has changed over time. Urban demographics have changed over time, with nonwhites and Hispanics replacing such "older" streams of ethnic immigrants as Italians and Irish, but urban areas are still filled with people with different political concerns. With some exceptions, urban areas have greater population density (i.e., the number of people per square mile) and a greater need for government services and support in various forms than suburban and rural areas. Urban areas are more likely to be populated by individuals who are minorities, renters, less affluent, and more in need of social programs. The exception is that some cities have large pockets of very affluent individuals who have less need for government programs. Despite these exceptions, central cities generally contain people with a greater need for government support.

To be able to track how Democrats have fared in urban areas over time, we need an indicator of urbanization. This analysis uses the population density of a House district because being "urban" does not differentiate districts as finely as density does. A "place" need have only 2,500 people to be urban, so a suburban area and a densely populated central city may both be designated as urban. Population density provides a better estimate of the extent to which an area is a heavily populated central city. Figure 3.8 tracks three indicators of the changing relationship between population density and Democratic success.[10] The

**Figure 3.8   Correlation of Population Density and Democratic Presidential–
House Percentages, and Difference in House Success by Density,
1900–2002**

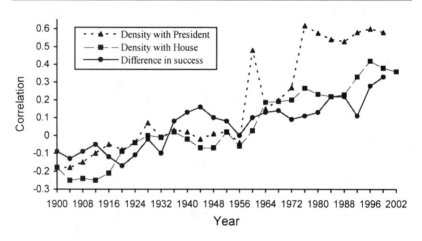

Source: Data compiled by the author.

figure presents the correlations of the population density of House districts with the Democratic percentage of the vote for presidential and
House candidates for each year. A positive correlation between population density and the Democratic presidential vote percentage indicates
that Democrats in that year received higher vote percentages in areas
with greater density. A negative correlation indicates that Democrats in
that year did worse in high-density districts.

In the early part of the twentieth century, the correlation of presidential and House vote percentages with density was negative, meaning
Democrats did relatively better in areas with low population density.
The correlation of votes with density then rose to around 0 (indicating
that the party's success was roughly the same in districts with low, moderate, and high population density levels) in 1928 and stayed at that
level for roughly the next thirty years. Beginning in the 1960s, the correlation started to increase.

The third line in Figure 3.8 tracks the differential (in percentage
points) in Democratic success in winning House seats between districts
with lower and higher levels of population density. In this case, higher
density districts are defined as those with at least 500 people per square
mile. The percentage of all House districts in this category increased

from 17 to 43 percent from 1900 to 2000. The "difference" represented by the third line is the percentage of seats won by Democrats in higher density districts minus those won in districts with lower levels of density. That is, if Democrats won 75 percent of higher-density districts and 40 percent of lower-density districts, the difference would be 35 percentage points, or 0.35. A negative number means Democrats did better in lower density districts, and a positive number indicates more success in districts with relatively high density. Democrats did not do relatively better in more dense districts until 1936. After that, they held a small advantage through the 1980 elections.

All three relationships shown in Figure 3.8 rose from the 1960s through the 2000 elections. Some of this may just reflect the increasing tendency of minorities to locate in urban areas. Blacks had been steadily migrating to urban areas in the North and South since the 1940s (Lemann, 1991), resulting in a greater nonwhite presence in urban areas (Stonecash et al., 2003: 72–73). Immigration was also increasing, with most immigrants locating in urban areas. The result was that the more urban areas of the country had large concentrations of immigrants and nonwhites, and these were areas where the population was less affluent, had less education, and was struggling with economic success. They were more likely to need government services and legislation to secure various job protections and rights.

The Democratic Party, which had a largely rural electoral base at the beginning of the century, now draws 60 percent of its seats from higher-density districts. The shift to greater reliance on urban areas, which began in the 1920s with Al Smith, has gradually and dramatically transformed the Democratic Party to one with a much more liberal voting record in Congress (Bond and Fleisher, 2000). The Reagan administration, which was seeking to cut social programs, provided a stark contrast with a Democratic Party that was gradually becoming more liberal. In addition, the growing polarization of the country (Jacobson, 2003a) has resulted in a steady increase in the correlation of density and Democratic success, as noted previously.

This pattern of an increase in the relationship between density and Democratic success, therefore, is not just a reflection of the decline of Democratic success in the South. The South has historically been less urban and more Democratic, so it might be that a decline in Democratic success in that region explains the change to a positive correlation between density and Democratic success. That is, the movement of rural areas to the Republican Party in the South over time may be the source of the present positive correlation. Figure 3.9 presents the correlations between density and Democratic vote percentages for the South and non-South. The pattern is the same within the two areas of the nation.

The Democratic Party's electoral reliance on nonwhites has also increased, although our ability to portray that transition is more difficult. In 1940, 77 percent of the nonwhite population in the United States lived in the South (Lemann, 1991: 6). Following the disenfranchisement efforts of the late 1800s (Kousser, 1974), almost all Southern blacks were prevented from registering and voting. Democrats won almost all Southern districts, including ones with a high percentage of nonwhites. But with Southern Democrats excluding blacks from voting booths, the 1900–1960 association between the percentage of nonwhites and Democratic success in winning House seats was very deceiving. Blacks were present, but they could not vote, and the elected representatives from these districts had very conservative, segregationist voting records.

Figure 3.9   Correlation of House District Population Density and Democratic Presidential–House Percentages, by Region, 1900–2000

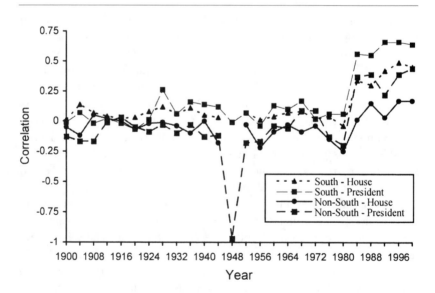

Source: Data compiled by the author.

The association between demographics and political outcomes began to take on real meaning as the 1960s unfolded. First, from the 1930s through the 1950s, blacks were migrating from the South to Northern urban areas, creating a growing electoral base outside the South that did vote. Second, those blacks remaining in the South were able to register in large numbers beginning in the mid-1960s. In those districts where blacks constituted a significant proportion of the electorate, their presence resulted in the election of relatively liberal Southern Democrats (Glaser, 1996). Further, the number of Hispanics immigrating into the United States has greatly increased. About one-half of Hispanics regard themselves as nonwhite or multiracial.[11]

Together, these two trends have changed the presence of nonwhites in US society and altered the electoral bases of the two parties. Table 3.1 presents the distribution of House districts in the last forty years by the percentage of the population within the district that is nonwhite, based on census data, using increments of 10 percentage points. Then the distribution of districts across the categories is first presented for each decade. For politics, the most important matter is the percentage of districts that have 20–30 percent or more nonwhites because Democrats have traditionally done much better in winning these districts. For example, in the 2002 election, 80 percent of House seats in districts with 30 percent or more nonwhites were won by Democrats. As the number of such districts grows, they provide more of a base for Democratic House candidates, and they become districts that a Democratic presidential candidate is more likely to win.

In the 1960s, 64.8 percent of all House districts had 10 percent or fewer nonwhites, and 12.6 percent had 30 percent or more nonwhites. Since then, the composition of districts has changed considerably. In 2002, only 23.2 percent of districts had 10 percent or fewer nonwhites, and 30.1 percent of districts had 30 percent or more nonwhites. These figures somewhat exaggerate the electoral impact of nonwhites because many of them are not yet naturalized citizens and many are not registered to vote. Nonetheless, the comparison between the figures for the 1960s and 2002 indicate how much the composition of the nation has changed. Nonwhites now constitute a larger percentage of US society.

While the composition of districts was changing, the long-term realignment of the parties was shifting their success within types of districts. In House elections, Democrats have continually won more than 80 percent of all seats in districts that are 30 percent or more nonwhite, as the second set of numbers in Table 3.1 shows. The major change has

Table 3.1   Distribution of House Districts by Percentage Nonwhite, and Democratic Success by Percentage Nonwhite, 1960s–2002

	Decade of Apportionment				

Percentage Distribution of House Districts by Percent Nonwhites

% Nonwhite	1960s	1970s	1980s	1990s	2002
0–9	64.8	61.6	44.8	40.6	23.2
10–19	13.1	18.5	24.9	24.6	27.4
20–29	9.4	7.4	15.4	16.8	19.3
30 plus	12.6	12.4	14.9	18.4	30.1

Percentage of Seats Won by Democrats in House Elections

% Nonwhite	1960s	1970s	1980s	1990s	2002
0–9	45.7	52.3	46.0	36.2	26.7
10–19	75.4	69.5	56.9	41.3	31.9
20–29	82.9	81.8	78.5	53.7	45.2
30 plus	89.8	83.3	87.7	89.8	80.2

Percentage of Vote Won by Democratic
Presidential Candidates Within House Districts

% Nonwhite	1960s	1970s	1980s	1990s	2000
0–9	52.5	40.8	40.4	41.7	44.1
10–19	54.8	44.0	39.3	44.2	47.4
20–29	48.7	48.1	46.2	45.4	46.8
30 plus	47.8	56.0	56.7	64.0	68.0

Source: Based on data compiled by the author from various data sources. See Appendix B for an explanation of the election results. For an explanation of the demographic data, see Jeffrey M. Stonecash et al., *Diverging Parties: Social Change, Realignment, and Party Polarization* (Boulder, Colo., Westview Press, 2003), Appendix, pp. 155–159.

Note: All results for House and presidential elections are grouped within a decade. The results for presidential elections, for example, are the average of the 1960, 1964, and 1968 results. For the analysis of House districts, years are grouped into decades (five sets of elections) based on the years following reapportionment according to census data. A census is conducted in years ending in 0. Because census data are not available until the end of the year ending in 1 or the beginning of the year ending in 2, new districts are not drawn and in place until sometime in the year ending in 2. Those districts are then in existence (except for legal challenges) for elections in the years ending in 2, 4, 6, 8, and 0. For example, the election years that constitute the 1970 decade are not 1970–1978, but 1972–1980.

been in the percentage of House Democrats in districts with less than 30 percent nonwhites. From the 1960s through 2002, the party has experienced a steady decline in success in winning House seats in those districts. In the districts with 90 percent or more whites, its success declined from 45.7 to 26.7 percent. In presidential elections, as shown in the third set of numbers in Table 3.1, the party has experienced an equally significant shift. Democrats did marginally better in the districts with fewer than 10 percent nonwhites in the 1960s. In the 2000 election, they did better in the districts with 30 percent or more nonwhites. The difference in the percentage of the vote won between the bottom and top categories (less than 10 and more than 30 percent) is now 23.9 percentage points, which is greater than any other decade.

The result has been a substantial increase in the Democratic Party's reliance on nonwhite constituents. The net effect of the registration of blacks, their movement to urban areas, and an increase in immigration is that there are now more districts with substantial percentages of non-whites, and the Democratic Party for both House and presidential elections now derives a greater percentage of its votes from these districts. In the 1960s, Democrats derived 33 percent of their seats from districts where nonwhites were 20 percent or more of the district. In the 2002 election, Democrats derived 69 percent of their seats from such districts (Stonecash, Brewer and Mariani, 2003: 51–106). In the span of 40 years, the increase in Democratic reliance on nonwhites has been dramatic. At the individual level, the percentage of votes for Democratic House and Senate members has steadily increased since the 1950s (Jacobson, 2000: 25).

The Emergence of New Bases of Political Divisions: Individual-Level Evidence

As new electoral divisions were developing for House districts, they were also emerging at the individual level. Political divisions by race, income, ideology, and religious attachment were also increasing. Blacks moved abruptly and strongly to support the Democratic Party immediately after the 1964 Civil Rights Act was proposed by President Lyndon Johnson and opposed by Republican presidential candidate Barry Goldwater (Carmines and Stimson, 1989). Blacks have voted heavily Democratic since then.

The emergence of political divisions by income was more gradual. In the 1950s, despite the presumption that the New Deal coalition was class based, divisions by income were fairly limited. By the 1970s, the difference in voting Democratic between those in the bottom and top thirds of the income distribution began to increase, and it continued to increase in the 1980s and 1990s (Stonecash, 2000). Table 3.2 presents the extent of division in party identification and voting by income groups in the past fifty years.

As the parties have continued to diverge on the broad ideological issue of whether government should intrude to remedy social problems, voters have responded by realigning according to their own ideologies.

Table 3.2 Income and Ideological Divisions: Percentage Voting and Identifying with Democrats, by Income and Ideological Groups, Whites Only, 1950s–2002

Decade[a] Income[b]:	Presidential Voting			House Election Voting			Party Identification		
	Low	High	Diff	Low	High	Diff	Low	High	Diff
1950s	42	38	4	56	48	8	55	51	4
1960s	49	47	2	56	52	4	54	51	3
1970s	42	33	9	61	49	12	53	45	8
1980s	46	30	16	62	48	14	53	40	13
1990–2002[c]	62	43	19	64	43	21	58	43	15
Change	20	5	15	8	−5	13	−1	−8	11
Ideology[d]	Lib	Cons	Diff	Lib	Cons	Diff	Lib	Cons	Diff
1970s	72	18	55	75	43	32	73	32	41
1980s	70	21	49	78	39	38	75	30	45
1990–2002[c]	82	28	54	78	27	51	81	26	55
Change	10	10	0	3	−12	19	8	−6	14

Sources: The data are taken from the NES Cumulative Data Files for 1952–2002; Warren Miller and the National Election Studies, American National Election Studies Cumulative Data File, 1948–2002 [Computer file]. 12th ICPSR version (Ann Arbor: University of Michigan, Center for Political Studies [producer], 2003; Ann Arbor: Inter-university Consortium for Political and Social Research [distributor], 2003); and the 2002 NES study.

Notes: Only whites are included because for the last several decades their behavior has been the primary concern. Numbers are the percentages indicating they either voted for Democrats in the presidential (vcf0705) and House elections (vcf0707), or identified with the Democratic party (vcf0303).

a. The percentages for each year within a decade are averaged. Decades are defined as: 1950s: 1952–1958; 1960s: 1960–1968; 1970s: 1970–1978; 1980s: 1980–1988; 1990–2002 is the years indicated.

b. The income groupings of low and high are the bottom and top thirds, respectively.

c. The 2002 survey provides groupings of income that allow the creation of categories similar to those used in previous years.

d. For the ideology response groupings, respondents were asked to identify themselves on a seven-point scale, with 1 being liberal and 7 being conservative. Those with scores of 4 are not shown. Scores of 1–3 were grouped as liberal (Lib), and those 5–7 were grouped as conservative (Cons).

This alignment can be assessed by first asking citizens whether they see themselves as liberal, moderate, or conservative, and then examining how they vote and with which party they identify. Questions about self-identified ideology were first asked in the 1970s. There was already a significant ideological division in presidential voting in the 1970s. There was less ideological division in House races and in party identification in the 1970s, but by the 1990s the division was consistent for both presidential and House elections as well as for party identification. In the last several decades, more conservatives have moved to the Republican Party, and more liberals to the Democratic Party (Abramowitz and Saunders, 1998; Jacobson, 2001; Schreckhise and Shields, 2003: 605).

Religious attachments have also come to play a greater role in dividing people politically. Secularists, or those who do not have religious beliefs or involvement in a church, are more inclined to support the Democratic Party, whereas those who attend religious services regularly are much more likely to support the Republican Party (Layman, 2001). Those who are pro-life on the abortion issue are more likely to support the Republican Party, and those who are pro-choice are becoming more supportive of the Democratic Party (Adams, 1997). Those who worry about moral decline and support traditional family structures (e.g., two heterosexual parents) are more supportive of Republicans (White, 2003: 79–116).

There are now multiple bases of partisan division, which tend to reinforce each other. Race, ideology, and income overlap to enough of an extent to reinforce each other and to strengthen the sense of difference among voters.

The Resurgence of Partisanship

As all these changes evolved, partisanship has reemerged at both the aggregate and individual levels. At the district level, the association between results for House and presidential candidates of the same party has increased. Figure 3.10 presents the correlation of these partisan results across the last century. This association was high through the first half of the century, dipped in 1948, bounced back somewhat in 1952 and 1956, then significantly declined again in 1960 and 1964, and has tended to climb since 1964.

A similar pattern has prevailed for individual-level behavior. An important indicator of partisanship is the extent to which individuals

Political Parties Matter

Figure 3.10 Correlation of Democratic House–Presidential Percentages for House Districts, 1900–2000

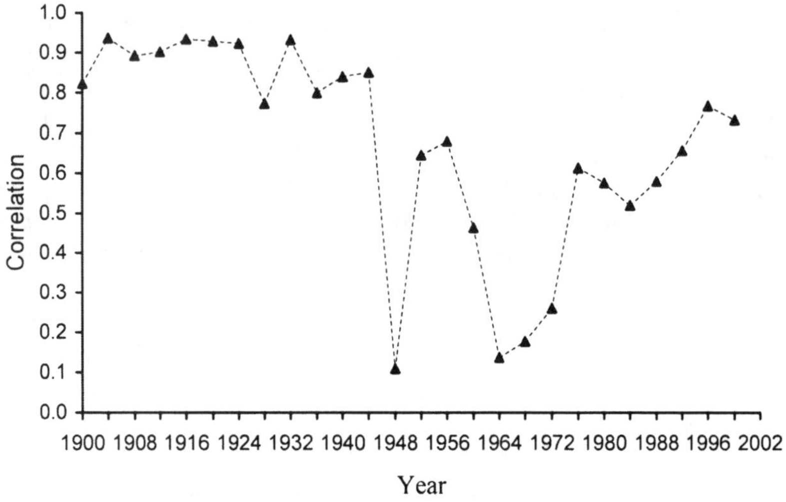

Source: Data compiled by the author.

who say they identify with a party actually vote for candidates of that party. Figure 3.11 presents the correlation for presidential years between party identification and voting for candidates of that party for 1952–2000. During the 1950s, the first years for which individual-level data are available, the correlation between party identification and presidential voting was above 65 percent. It then dipped (with erratic movements) through the late 1960s and into the early 1980s, and then rose in 1996 and 2000. The pattern for House candidates is similar, with a decline throughout the 1960s and 1970s and then a rise in the 1980s and 1990s.

A Changed Party?

Does the return of partisanship to its previous level in the last decade or so constitute a "restoration" of the past? Was the decline in partisanship surrounding the 1970s just a lull in partisanship, a temporary deviation from an essentially stable situation due to the political turmoil of the 1960s and 1970s?

Figure 3.11   Percentage of Major Party Identifiers Voting for Candidates of Their Party, 1952–2000

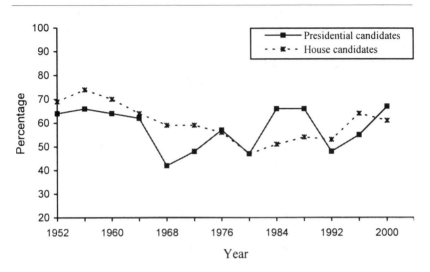

Source: NES Cumulative Data File, 1948–2002.
Note: Only years with both presidential and House elections appear.

The indicators of partisanship suggest a return to prior conditions, but this surface similarity hides fundamental changes in the parties' electoral bases. If there is a constant in the situation of the parties, it is that Democrats have remained the relatively liberal party and Republicans have remained the relatively conservative party. Congressional voting records are a useful guide to the positions of the parties over time. Poole and Rosenthal (1984, 1985, 1991, 1997) have analyzed all votes of members in the House and have created an index of the ideological position of members, called "DW-Nominate scores," which range from roughly −1 to +1. A negative score indicates a member was consistently very liberal, whereas a positive score indicates a consistent conservative position. Their results indicate that the Democratic Party has been consistently liberal on economic issues. Although the opposition to civil rights by conservative Southern Democrats in the 1940s to the 1960s certainly pushed some party members away from a consistently liberal position, Democrats have traditionally been more willing to use the government to address economic and social problems. In the early 1900s, that position involved efforts to regulate the private sector, including labor legislation to help protect workers (James, 2000; Sanders, 1999). In the 1930s, it involved the New Deal legislation to provide public works and social security. In the 1960s and 1970s, it involved support for numerous social programs. In the 1980s and 1990s, the party became more concerned with protecting existing social programs and preventing large tax cuts (particularly for the affluent), which would reduce federal government revenues and make it difficult to maintain social programs.

That consistency is evident in the association of House voting records with Democratic votes. Figure 3.12 presents the correlation of DW-Nominate scores for House members with the Democratic percentage of the vote for House and presidential candidates for each year. Because a more liberal House member will have a negative DW-Nominate score, a negative correlation indicates that the lower the score (more liberal), the higher the Democratic percentage of the vote. Throughout the last 100 years, the pattern has been that the House districts in which legislators have the most liberal voting records are also the ones where Democrat House and presidential candidates have received the highest vote percentages. In other words, districts with strong voting support for Democrats have consistently yielded House

Figure 3.12   Correlation of DW-Nominate Scores with Democratic House–Presidential Results and Density, 1900–2000

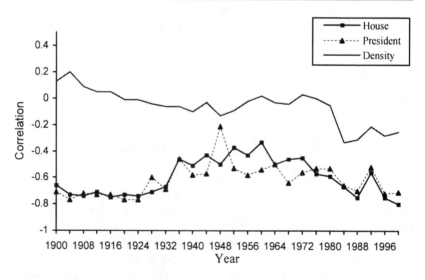

Source: Election results and density data compiled by the author; DW-Nominate scores taken from the web site of Keith Poole, http://www.voteview.com.

members with liberal voting records. This relationship weakened from the 1930s through the 1970s, when issues of race and the role in providing social programs gained dominance, but there was still considerable overall stability for 100 years in the relationship of liberal voting in Congress and electoral support for Democrats.

This apparent stability, however, conceals considerable change in the geographical electoral bases of the parties. From 1900 to 1948, the party did better in more rural districts, and the most liberal voting records came from those districts. Over time this relationship has reversed, and now the most liberal voting records are associated with the districts with the greatest population density. Figure 3.12 also presents the correlation of DW-Nominate scores for House members with the population density in a district (the population of a district divided by its area in square miles). In the early 1900s, the correlation was positive, indicating that the most liberal voting records (a negative number) occurred in the districts with the lowest density. Put another way, the most conservative voting records occurred in the districts with the highest density, creating a positive correlation until about 1932. That correlation has gradually turned negative since then, indicating that now the most liberal voting records are found in the districts with the highest population density.

The Democratic dominance in the South has disappeared. In 2000, Democrats did better outside the South than in the South in both presidential and House elections. The region that had been the most Democratic now provides the strongest support for Republican presidential candidates. The non-Southern states, which were the most Republican in 1900, are now more Democratic. As Table 3.3 indicates, Democratic presidential candidates in 1900 received 43.2 percent of votes outside the South, and in 2000 they received 45.8 percent. In House races outside the South, Democrats received 44.0 percent in 1900 and 52.2 percent in 2000.

In 1900, Democrats received 63.6 percent of their electoral votes from the South, but in 2000 they received 0 percent. In 1900, they derived 54.1 percent of their House seats from the South, and by 2000 this percentage was down to 25.1 percent, even as the South was becoming home to a higher percentage of the US population. Democrats now also derive more of their electoral votes from outside the South, and a much higher percentage of their seats come from outside the South.

Even though indicators of partisanship, such as the correlation of presidential and House results, may suggest the past has returned, the alignment underlying this correlation is now very different from that in 1900. It is not just that the geographical bases of the parties are different. Race is now a major source of differences in partisanship, whereas it was modest in the 1950s. Class divisions were muted in the 1950s but are now growing.[13] Liberals and conservatives are more divided in their support for the parties, and religious attitudes now divide people more. Partisanship has returned but with greater differences in who supports each party. The important matter is how voters have reacted to all these changes.

Table 3.3 A Shifted Political Order: Democratic Success in 1900 and 2000

	South	Non-South
President		
1900		
Percentage of electoral votes won	100.0	12.8
Average percentage of vote won	67.6	43.2
Percentage of electoral votes from	63.6	36.4
2000		
Percentage of electoral votes won	0	68.6
Average percentage of vote won	43.3	45.8
Percentage of electoral votes from	0	100.0
Change 1900 to 2000		
Percentage of electoral votes won	−100.0	55.8
Average percentage of vote won	−24.3	2.6
Percentage of electoral votes from	−63.6	63.6
House Districts		
1900		
Percentage of seats won	95.6	27.3
Average percentage of vote won	73.5	44.0
Percentage of seats from	54.1	45.9
2000		
Percentage of seats won	40.5	52.0
Average percentage of vote won	44.5	52.2
Percentage of seats from	25.1	74.9
Change 1900 to 2000		
Percentage of seats won	−55.1	24.7
Average percentage of vote won	−31.7	8.2
Percentage of seats from	−29.0	29.0

Source: Jerrold G. Rusk, *A Statistical History of the American Electorate* (Washington, D.C.: Congressional Quarterly Press, 2001). For 1900: p. 139 (presidential popular vote), p. 141 (electoral votes), p. 233 (House votes), and p. 260 (seats won). For 2000, see "2000 Presidential General Election Results," available at http://www.fec.gov/pubrec/fe2000/2000presge.htm.

4

Changing Party Compositions and Voter Response

The shifts in the electoral bases of the two major political parties over the last century have created considerable change for the parties. The central concern of the analysis presented here is how these changes affected partisan attachments of the electorate in the last fifty years. The evidence indicates that partisanship at the aggregate and individual levels were fairly strong during the 1950s, declined through the 1960s and 1970s, and began to rise after that. How does realignment explain that pattern?

To repeat the argument presented earlier, this transition in electoral bases first created a decline and then a rise in partisanship. The transition had two specific effects that lowered partisanship. First, as the transition occurred, the parties became more diverse internally, creating considerable ambiguity about the extent to which the parties differed. The decline in partisanship was not just a reaction to political turmoil, but reflected reactions to parties with less distinct differences, resulting in less imperative to identify with a party. A second, seemingly contradictory effect was that other voters were moving away from their existing partisan attachments and changing party identification because they perceived that the parties were changing their policy concerns and positions. Democrats were beginning to show more concern for civil rights, women, and issues of redistribution. Republicans were reducing their support for civil rights, government activism, and taxation. Those shifts were creating realignments. Liberals within the Republican Party were finding their party less hospitable, and likewise, conservatives within the Democratic Party were finding their party less hospitable.

As those uncomfortable with their connections moved away from their parties, they first moved to the independent category, creating a decline in partisanship. This change, however, was not an indicator of a decline in the significance of parties and a rejection of future partisanship. Rather, this behavior reflected a rejection of one party and the beginning of realignment. It was the first step toward a renewal of parties and a partisan identity that better fit with the voters' own views. None of these changes occurred quickly, and they are surely still evolving (Aldrich, 2003). As the transition continued, the differences between the two parties and the direction of each party became clearer, and partisanship began to increase. More people saw a difference between the parties and a reason to make a choice. Those uncomfortable with their current party continued to gradually move to the other. As this movement evolved, stronger partisanship returned.

These changes were probably more complicated than that. Some voters—the more attentive and more ideological—are likely to have detected the shifts in party concerns more quickly, and they may have been the first to consider changing their party identifications if they sensed a conflict between their positions and the direction of the parties with which they currently identified. Those who were less attentive probably lagged. Others, with weakly formed opinions on some issues, may have adjusted their views according to their party identification (Layman and Carsey, 2002a). New, younger entrants into the political process who replaced older cohorts probably struggled to sort out the party differences for some time, leading to more independents. The essential point is that transition created a sorting out, which ultimately resulted in a renewal of partisanship.

Changing Party Compositions

Just how much was the composition of parties changing during the last fifty years? These changes within and between the parties can be tracked by using diverse data sources. One commonly used indicator of the relative positions of the congressional parties is the average Americans for Democratic Action (ADA) score for each party. The ADA is a liberal group that chooses a set of bills for each session and designates a proper liberal vote and then scores each legislator as to how they voted. A score of 100 indicates a completely liberal score, and a 0 indicates a completely conservative score. Figure 4.1 tracks the average ADA scores for House Democrats and Republicans since 1948,

Figure 4.1   Average ADA Ratings, by Party, US House, 1948–2000

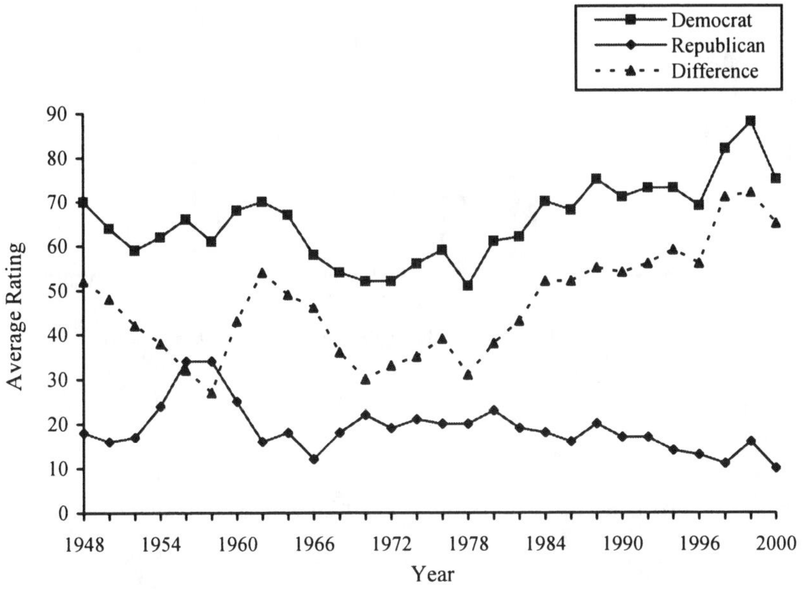

Source: Data taken from the files of Americans for Democratic Action and their web site.

along with the differences between the two. In 1948, the difference was relatively large. It then declined until 1958, rose again, but was relatively low throughout the 1970s. Then, in 1980, the difference began to steadily widen. The important matter is that, with some fluctuations, the late 1960s and 1970s were a time of diminished differences between the parties.

The difference between the two parties declined in the 1960s and 1970s because each party acquired more moderates during that time. The DW-Nominate scores (see Chapter 3) provide an indication of the distribution of members within each party over time.[14] Figures 4.2 through 4.4 indicate the distribution of party members in 1900, 1976, and 2000, respectively. The starting point for the parties in this analysis is 1900. The year 1976 is in the midst of the party transition in electoral bases, and 2000 represents the end point of much of this analysis. In the coding of legislators' voting records, a negative score is a liberal voting record, and a positive score is a conservative record. In 1900, there was very little overlap in voting records, and Democrats were distributed to

Figure 4.2   Distribution of Democrats and Republicans by DW-Nominate Scores, 1900

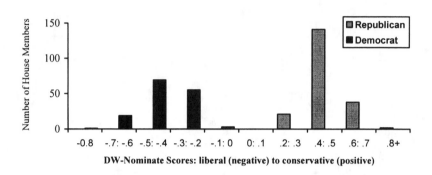

Source: DW-Nominate scores taken from the web site of Keith Poole, http://www. voteview.com.

Figure 4.3   Distribution of Democrats and Republicans by DW-Nominate Scores, 1976

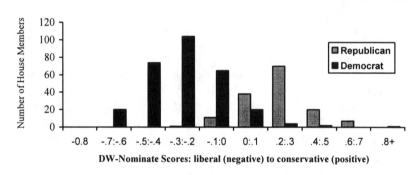

Source: DW-Nominate scores taken from the web site of Keith Poole, http://www. voteview.com.

the left and Republicans to the right along the liberal-conservative continuum. By 1976, the distributions of scores for each party had moved more toward the middle, and there was considerable overlap between the two parties. That is, some Republicans had voting records more liberal than some Democrats and some Democrats had voting records more conservative than Republicans. By 2000, the distributions for each party had once again moved more to the left and right. There were very

Figure 4.4   Distribution of Democrats and Republicans by DW-Nominate Scores, 2000

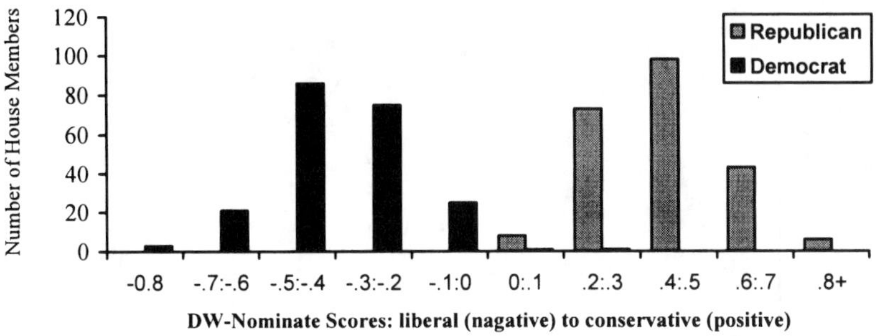

Source: DW-Nominate scores taken from the web site of Keith Poole, http://www. voteview.com.

few members in the middle, and the overlap between the two parties had almost vanished.

The overlap that prevailed in the 1970s is important. Greater overlap diminishes the sense of difference between the parties and the imperative for voters to choose one party over the other. Figure 4.5 provides year-by-year data on the extent to which the phenomenon of overlap occurred in the House over the last century. If a Democratic House member was more conservative (i.e., had a higher score) than any Republican member, the member was coded as overlapping. Republicans who were more liberal (i.e., had a lower score) than any Democrat were coded as overlapping. This is an undemanding definition of overlap, but it is useful to allow us to track change.

The number of party members who overlapped with the other party rose steadily from the 1940s through the 1970s. The result was that coalitions of Democrats and Republicans were often more significant than divisions between the parties. Southern Democrats often joined with Republicans on conservative legislation, and liberal, non-Southern Republicans often voted with non-Southern Democrats (Brady, Cooper and Hurley, 1979; Collie and Brady, 1985; Rohde, 1991: 9–16).

Beginning in the 1970s, the extent of overlap began to decline, and now, in the early 2000s, there is almost no overlap.[15] There are now fewer and fewer moderates in the House and the Senate (Fleisher and Bond, 2004),[16] which results in very little overlap between the parties.

These same DW-Nominate scores allow us to track the shifting

**Figure 4.5   House Members with Voting Records Overlapping Other Party,
            1900–2000**

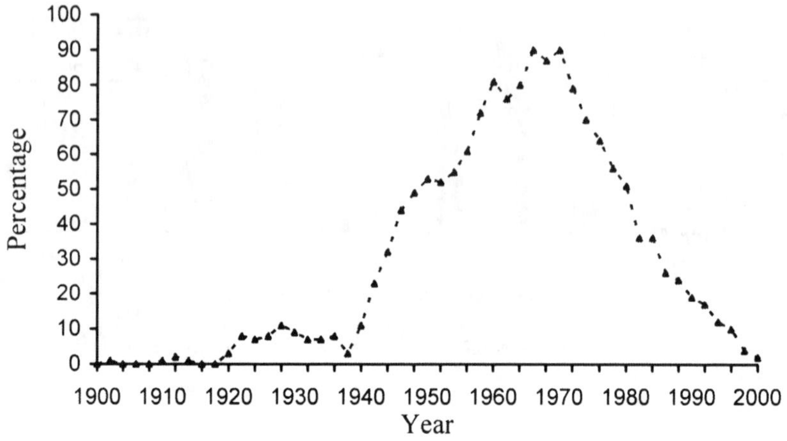

Source: Election results compiled by the author; DW-Nominate scores taken from the web site of Keith Poole, http://www.voteview.com.

composition of the parties over time. For these graphs, a liberal is coded as –1.0 to less than –0.2, a moderate is –0.2 to 0.2, and a conservative is greater than 0.2 to 1.0. This coding is largely arbitrary and is intended to compare voting records in a consistent way over time. Even acknowledging that caution must be applied in interpreting results, Figures 4.6 and 4.7 indicate clear changes in the composition of the parties over time.

As discussed earlier, the Democratic Party experienced change before the Republicans did. The realignment of the 1930s brought a large number of moderates into the Democratic Party. That created a coalition with tensions between the liberal and moderate wings of the party, and it was a tension that persisted through the 1960s and 1970s. Those House districts that had more conservative members eventually elected Republicans, reducing the role of conservatives within the Democratic Party and increasing the dominance of relative liberals within the party.

The Republican Party was largely dominated by conservatives for the first 40 years of the twentieth century. Despite that, the party had always had some Eastern liberals and some moderates scattered around the country. The relative role of these moderate Republicans increased

Figure 4.6   Distribution of House Democratic Members' Voting Records, 1900–2000

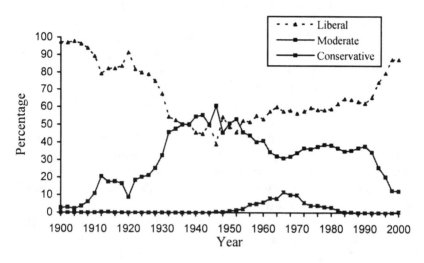

Source: Election results and density data compiled by the author; DW-Nominate scores taken from the web site of Keith Poole, http://www.voteview.com.

Figure 4.7   Distribution of House Republican Members' Voting Records, 1900–2000

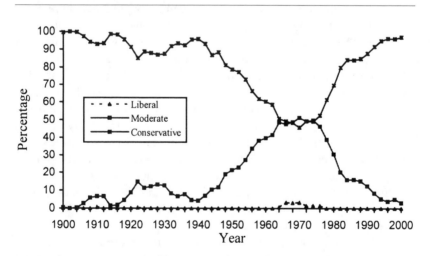

Source: Election results and density data compiled by the author; DW-Nominate scores taken from the web site of Keith Poole, http://www.voteview.com.

during the 1950s and into the 1970s, when the party was comprised of almost equal proportions of conservatives and moderates. The result was considerable tension within the party. It was during this time that conservatives began their sustained efforts to assert much more power within the party. As conservatives acquired more influence during the 1980s, moderates were gradually displaced in the Republican Party by conservatives. Moderates declined steadily thereafter, and presently there are very few in the party.

The years surrounding the 1970s, then, were ones in which the diversity within each party increased, the average party member was more moderate, and there was considerable overlap among party members. This was an era in which voters were less likely to see significant differences between the parties and less likely to have a clear image of the policy positions of each party because of their internal diversity. If voters identify with parties because they see a significant difference between the parties, and see a reason to identify with one rather than another, then the greater intraparty diversity and the declining differences between the parties during the 1970s should have produced a decrease in identification with parties.

But the era that produced more independents was also an era that contained the beginnings of changes that would lead many voters to reassess their party attachments and perhaps change their party identifications. The result would be a renewed attachment to parties. That transition was neither quick nor easy, but it eventually produced more clearly defined parties. For each party, the transition resulted in declining dominance by the region that had been their primary base in the early 1900s. As party positions evolved, their earlier core regional bases were not inclined to support the new direction of the party, and they acted as moderates within the party. As the transition occurred, Southern Democrats were reluctant to go along with a more liberal national Democratic Party (Aldrich, 2003) and held out with relatively moderate voting positions. They were eventually replaced by Republicans or more liberal Democrats (Black and Black, 2002). As the Republican Party shifted its base out of the North, House members from that region continued to vote as moderates during the transition until they were replaced by more conservative Republicans or liberal Democrats (Stonecash, Brewer, and Mariani, 2002).

Figure 4.8 tracks the changes in the relative presence of three crucial groups in the Republican Party: Northern conservatives, Northern moderates, and Southern conservatives. Through the 1950s, Northern conservatives constituted the bulk of the party, with very few Northern

Figure 4.8   Composition of House Republican Party, 1900–2000

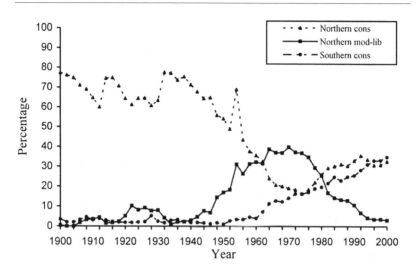

Source: Election results compiled by the author; DW-Nominate scores taken from the web site of Keith Poole, http://www.voteview.com.

Note: North is defined here as those states running westward from Maine to Minnesota and southward to, but not including, those states that constitute the South. Specifically, this includes Maine, New Hampshire, Vermont, Massachusetts, Connecticut, Rhode Island, New York, New Jersey, Delaware, Maryland, West Virginia, Pennsylvania, Ohio, Indiana, Illinois, Michigan, Wisconsin, and Minnesota.

moderates and almost no Southern conservatives. Later in the 1950s, Northern moderates began to increase and displace Northern conservatives. Then, in the 1960s, Southern conservatives began to emerge as a crucial part of the party. As the 1960s and 1970s progressed, approximately 70 percent of the party was composed of these three groups, with no regional group having dominance. This transition era resulted in a muddled image of the Republican Party. Then, in the 1980s, Southern conservatives steadily rose as a percentage of the party, and Northern moderates declined, followed by a resurgence of Northern conservatives. By the 1990s, Northern moderates were disappearing within the party, creating more of a consistent image of a conservative party.

The Democratic Party was also experiencing a changing composition, with regional shifts playing a major role. Figure 4.9 presents the changes within the Democratic Party. For the first part of the century, 50 to 70 percent of the members were Southern Democrats with liberal voting records. Northern liberals provided another 20 percent of the

Figure 4.9   Composition of House Democratic Party, 1900–2000

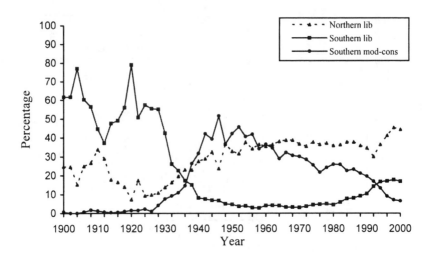

Source: Election results and density data compiled by the author; DW- Nominate scores taken from the web site of Keith Poole, http://www.voteview.com.

party. That composition changed in the 1930s as Northern liberals became a larger portion of the party. Southern Democrats, troubled by the issue of a growing federal role and legislation that might protect blacks and disrupt the Southern way of life, began to move toward more conservative positions (Reiter, 2001).

During the 1940s through the 1960s the Democratic Party was a diverse coalition, with as many Southern conservatives as Northern liberals. The tensions between these two wings were sharp and persistent and were made more intense when issues such as civil rights of Southern blacks were raised. The results of specific elections also created tension. The 1958 and 1964 House elections brought large numbers of liberal Democrats into the party. These liberals were faced with a House party in which conservative Southern Democrats held most committee chairs and resisted passing any liberal legislation (Polsby, 2004: 7–74). The party's composition was becoming more liberal. It was not, however, a unified party that could pass liberal legislation to define itself to the electorate.

Since the 1940s, the presence of Southern Democrats with moderate-conservative records has steadily declined. In some cases, these Democrats were replaced by conservative Republicans. In other districts, with the registration of minorities and the emergence of class divisions in the South (Brewer and Stonecash, 2001), more liberal Democrats began to win seats in the South. Liberals from all regions of the nation began to dominate the party, and its voting record moved steadily liberal.

Together, all these transitions changed the electoral bases of the parties. Parties that had been defined in large part by their regional bases and the accompanying issues had become parties in which their supporters increasingly differed in race, class, ideology, and religious attachments. As the parties have diverged in their electoral bases, party conflicts over policy have become more pronounced. Party members have also been willing to give their leaders in Congress more power to induce members to act cohesively in voting (Rohde, 1991). That, in turn, has increased conflict in Congress, pushing party members further apart and increasing the perceived differences between the parties (Jacobson, 2004). As the conflict escalates, party activists are more motivated to seek to mobilize their supporters to help win elections. Both parties are, of course, also trying to persuade moderates that their party approach is better for the nation, but the focus on mobilizing their electoral base has been significant.

Voters eventually realize these differences, although with some delay. Voters are generally not absorbed with politics (Popkin, 1994), but messages about party differences eventually reach them. If so, then the percentage of the electorate perceiving a difference between the parties and caring about which party wins should increase. Survey data covering 1952 through 2000 allow us to track the electoral perceptions of the parties. Figure 4.10 indicates the percentage of the electorate that sees a significant difference between the parties and the percentage that cares who wins the presidential race. In the 1950s, approximately 50 percent of the survey respondents saw a difference between the parties. That percentage then dipped modestly in 1972 and 1976, but then rose from 1980 through 2000. The same pattern occurred for responses to the question about caring who wins the presidential contest. The percentage who cared dipped in 1972, 1976, and 1980, but it has increased steadily since then. The changes in parties and their concerns have been gradually recognized by the electorate.

As awareness has increased, issues have come to play a greater role in the polarization of the electorate. A greater number of issues now divide voters and the parties. The scope of issues that create conflict has expanded (Brewer, 2004). Also, those who are consistently liberal or

Figure 4.10   Voter Reactions to Elections, 1952–2000

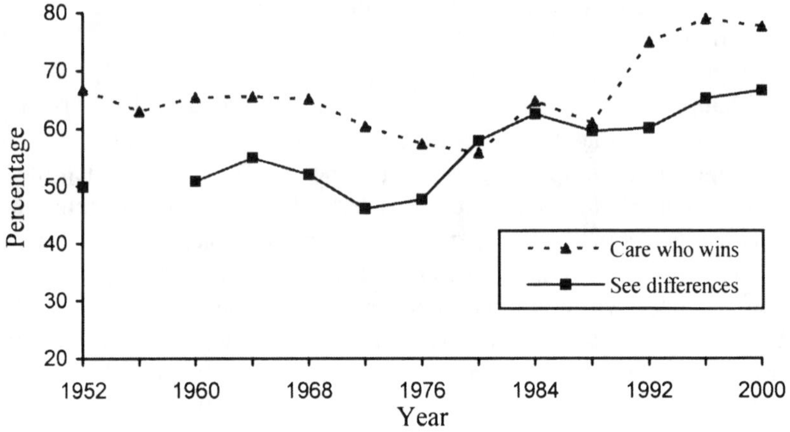

Source: NES Cumulative Data File, 1948–2002.

conservative are more likely to hold different views of the parties (Carmines and Ensley, 2004).

To summarize, these transitions in party bases during the last century have two implications for voters' attachments to parties. The transitions temporarily diminished the differences between the parties during the 1960s and 1970s, resulting in an increase in self-identified independents and independent voting behavior. But that same transition created the basis for a renewal of partisanship. The declines in partisanship that were so widely interpreted as the demise of parties were really the beginnings of a re-sorting of the electorate and renewed partisanship.

The intent of the remaining chapters is to assess the extent to which the appearance of declining attachment to parties was largely a product of these transitions in party electoral bases. Considerable evidence exists at the aggregate and individual levels that the resurgence of partisanship in the last decade or so is tied to realignment. The question is how changes from the 1950s through the 1980s reduced partisan attachments but also created a basis for their renewal. The subsequent chapters focus on changes in three crucial indicators of partisanship: split outcomes in House districts, and then the individual-level changes of the rise and fall of split-ticket voting and independents.

5

Split Outcomes in House Districts

The first suggestions that partisan attachments were declining came from aggregate data. Burnham (1965), using aggregate state and county level data, found a steady rise in the extent of ticket-splitting from 1900 through 1960 (pp. 13–20). There was also a steady decline in the similarity of results for different offices at the county and state levels. Others found that the percentage of House districts with split outcomes for presidential and House votes was steadily increasing (Jones, 1964: 465; Cummings, 1966: 31–39; Burnham, 1975: 428). "Split outcomes" refer to cases in which one party wins the presidential vote within the district and the other party wins the House seat. As Figure 5.1 indicates, the first half of the century experienced few such split outcomes, and the correlation of presidential and House results was very high. Then, in 1948, the presence of split outcomes began to rise, along with a corresponding decline in the correlation between House and presidential vote percentages for House districts.

The decline-of-partisanship view of these trends was plausible because political conditions were changing in a way that would create this development. Incumbent members of the House had larger staffs, more campaign funds, and greater access to polling and political consultants to help them present themselves. The percentage of close elections was declining, and the argument was plausible that declining

An earlier version of this chapter was presented at the 2003 American Political Science Association Meetings, Philadelphia, August–September, 2003

**Figure 5.1   House–Presidential Results: Correlation and Percentage with
Split Outcomes, 1900–2000**

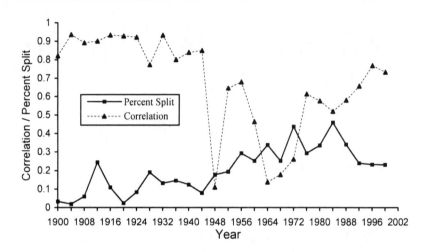

Source: Data compiled by the author. See Appendix B.

competitiveness in House races and increasing split outcomes were
both a result of the greater resources available to incumbents (Mayhew,
1974a: 297–304; 1974b: 27). The argument was that incumbents were
able to exploit their increased staff and office budgets to promote a
personal image that was separate from their party and the president
(Jacobson, 2001). This would allow House members to avoid being
tied to swings in presidential support. The result would be candidate-
centered rather than party-centered campaigns, such that the election
results for members could diverge from that for their presidential candidate. This would explain the increase in split outcomes and the
decline in the correlation between presidential and House results that is
evident in Figure 4.1.

   The difficulty with this argument is that while a consensus was
developing about the emergence of candidate-centered politics and the
decline of partisan attachments (Fiorina, 2002: 94–103), the trends
began to reverse. The percentage of districts with split outcomes began
to decline in 1988 and is now at the level that prevailed in 1948 and
1952. The correlation between House and presidential results began to
rise in 1964, and for the elections of 1992–2000 it was close to that
which existed in the 1930s and 1940s. The percentage of states with

split Senate partisanship in their delegations rose and fell from the 1940s through the 1990s (Burnell and Grofman, 1998: 394). These are not the trends one would expect if candidate-centered politics is dominant.[17] Although candidates continue to raise more money and to have access to large congressional office budgets, the trends in Figure 5.1 are now going in the opposite direction from what we might expect. If candidates continue to have access to more resources that give them the ability to create results divergent from that of their party's presidential candidate, the percentage of split outcomes should at least stay the same and probably increase.

The rise and fall of split outcomes is not just a reflection of the political transitions in the South, as Grofman et al. (2000) have suggested. Figure 5.2 presents the percentage of split outcomes within the South and the remainder of the nation. The presence of split outcomes has been somewhat greater in the South than in the rest of the nation, but the rise and fall in this percentage has been a nationwide phenomenon. Indeed, as Table 5.1 indicates, the majority of split outcomes since 1952 have occurred outside the South. The pattern of a rise and fall in split outcomes is the same in the South and outside the South. The presence of split outcomes rose during the 1960s through the 1980s and then declined in the 1990s.

Figure 5.2   Percentage of House Districts with Split House–Presidential Outcome, South and Non-South, 1900–2000

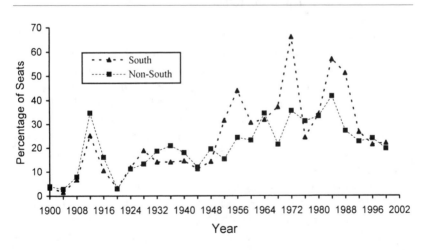

Source: Data compiled by the author.

Table 5.1　Split Outcomes for the Nation and by Region, 1952–2000

							Source of Split Outcomes	
	Percentage of Districts with Split Outcomes Within:							
	Nation		Non-South		South		Percentage of all from:	
Year	Number	Percent	Number	Percent	Number	Percent	Non-South	South
1952	84	19.5	49	15.3	35	31.0	58.3	41.7
1956	128	29.4	78	24.3	50	43.9	49.4	50.6
1960	109	25.1	75	23.2	35	30.7	68.8	31.2
1964	147	33.8	111	34.5	36	31.9	75.5	24.5
1968	111	25.5	69	21.4	42	37.2	62.2	37.8
1972	190	43.7	114	35.6	76	66.1	60.0	40.0
1976	128	29.4	100	31.3	28	24.4	78.1	21.9
1980	146	33.6	107	33.4	39	34.2	73.3	26.7
1984	200	46.0	130	41.7	70	56.9	65.0	35.0
1988	148	34.0	85	27.2	63	51.2	57.4	42.6
1992	104	23.9	69	22.7	35	26.7	66.3	33.7
1996	101	23.2	73	24.0	28	21.4	72.3	27.7
2000	89	20.5	60	19.7	29	22.1	67.4	32.6

Comparing Candidate-Centered and Realignment Explanations of Change

The rise and fall of split outcomes presents the first puzzle in trying to understand what is happening to partisanship. There are essentially two possible explanations of this trend. One argument is that we are now in an era of candidate-centered campaigns and election outcomes, which should presumably create a decline in partisan attachments in the electorate. The other argument is that this rise in split outcomes reflects realignment and the transitional consequences of the presidential and House results not moving together (Burnell and Grofman, 1998).[18] Each of these has a plausible logic, and each generates a different expectation of what changes we should see over time. Before moving to relevant evidence, the changes that each argument should create need to be articulated more precisely.

The essence of the candidate-centered interpretation of campaigns is that House incumbents are seeking to create a personal connection with voters to affect voting results. Incumbents seek to become highly visible with favorable personal ratings.[19] If successful, this should produce greater support within the district, and a vote less tied to fluctuations in voting for presidential candidates.[20] Incumbents should be capable of creating this connection because they can use the resources of their office to respond to constituency needs; to advertise their presence and accomplishments through the press, newsletters, and mailings; and to schedule appearances at local meetings (Mayhew, 1974b: 306–313; Jacobson, 2001: 21–55). Incumbents can also exploit their position to raise money from those interested in the progress of legislation, providing them with more resources to present themselves to voters through direct mail and media ads. If they do this well, incumbents should be able to create a vote percentage that is higher and that differs from that of their party's presidential candidate.[21]

If incumbents are able to increase their vote percentage, we could see two kinds of effects. First, all incumbents might be able to separate their vote from that of their party's presidential vote. If the ability to make this separation increases over time, we should see a general rise in the vote difference between the vote for the incumbents and that for their party's presidential candidate, regardless of the percentage of the vote received by presidential candidates. As an alternative, the efforts of incumbents to distance themselves from the normal votes for a presidential candidate in their districts might be selective. It might be that those incumbents facing a close presidential vote in their districts will be most concerned with separating themselves from the presidential vote. If a presidential race is likely to be 50–50, no incumbents would wish to be tied to the outcome. Split outcomes have historically been most frequent in cases where presidential outcomes were close (Cummings, 1966: 50–53). If incumbents in this situation are the most inclined to separate themselves from presidential results, the greatest increases in divergence of votes should occur in districts where presidential elections are close.[22]

Figure 5.3 presents these two hypothetical patterns graphically, and Table 5.2 presents hypothetical percentages. In the figure, the thick line represents the variation in vote percentages for House candidates if their votes were a reflection of presidential results. The line for House Candidates-A, which runs first below and then above the presidential line, represents what House Democratic candidates (mostly, but not just Democratic incumbents) could achieve. The lines to the left represent cases in which Republican incumbents are likely to predominate (weak Democratic districts). In these cases, Republican incumbents should be able to do better than the Republican presidential vote, so they can hold a Democratic challenger below what the Democratic presidential candi-

Figure 5.3   Hypothetical Patterns of Divergence of House Candidate Votes from Democratic Presidential Candidate Votes

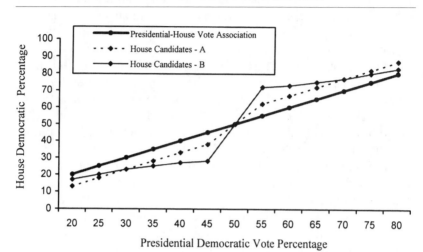

date receives. The result is an average Democratic House candidate vote below the presidential pattern.

Democratic incumbents will generally be to the right (strong Democratic districts), where districts are likely to be more Democratic and give Democratic presidential and House candidates higher percentages. If Democratic incumbents can uniformly increase their percentages above that of the presidential line, then Democratic incumbents should be able to create a vote percentage consistently higher than the presidential vote.

As an alternative, the movements away from presidential results might be located primarily at the center, where close presidential outcomes occur. Those candidates at the left and right extremes might be content to be tied to the presidential vote. A Democratic incumbent at the far right might be content to receive the same vote percentage as the Democratic presidential candidate (80 percent), and a Republican incumbent at the far left might be content to receive the same vote percentage as the Republican presidential candidate (80 percent at the extreme left). The most powerful incentive to move the House vote may occur in those districts where the presidential vote is close (around 50 percent). If efforts by Democratic incumbents (just to the right of 50 percent) and Republican incumbents (just to the left of 50 percent) are successful, then the divergences would be greater in the middle (the line for House Candidates-B). If incumbents are getting better at moving their vote, then the bulge of divergences around 50 percent would become greater over time.

These possibilities are summarized by using hypothetical percentages in Table 5.2. The first row (the 1950s) presents a hypothetical starting point and indicates what might have prevailed in the 1950s, when split outcomes were relatively low. The second row presents the average difference if there is a relatively uniform increase in the divergence of House candidate results from presidential results over time. The third row presents the average divergence if only incumbents faced with close presidential outcomes are concerned with, and successful at, moving their vote away from the presidential vote. If a pattern of general change occurred, then there would be a general rise in split outcomes across all groups of presidential results. If the change is selective, then there should be increases primarily in the middle three groups, or those in which presidential results are closer.

The alternative explanation of change is that the rise of split outcomes reflected the consequences of realignment. When presidential

Table 5.2   Alternative Hypothetical Patterns of House–Presidential Candidate Vote Divergence

	Democratic Presidential Candidate Percentage[a]				
	0–29	30–39	40–60	61–69	70–100

Democratic House–presidential candidate differences (incumbents present)

	Mostly Republicans			Mostly Democrats	
1950s	− 5	− 5	0	5	5
General change	−10	−10	0	10	10
Selective change	−10	−15	0	15	10

Notes: The numbers represent the average percentage point difference of House candidates from the presidential score within each district for cases in which an incumbent is present in the race.

a. For districts in which the Democratic presidential candidate received less than 40 percent of the vote, most of the incumbents are likely to be Republican incumbents who are able to hold a Democratic opponent to less than the level received by the presidential candidate, so the difference is negative. In districts where the Democratic presidential candidate received more than 60 percent of the vote, the House candidate is likely to be a Democrat and run ahead of the presidential candidate, so the number is positive. The middle category (40–60 percent) is likely to include both Republican and Democratic incumbents, resulting in a canceling of negative and positive differences and no net difference for incumbents.

candidates are part of a minority party, they seek new constituencies to create a majority coalition. In doing so, they are likely to articulate views different from their party's traditional policy positions and to seek votes in areas currently dominated by the majority party (James, 2000). If voters in these areas respond to this message and vote for the minority presidential candidate, but continue for some time to elect incumbents from the majority party, the result will be split outcomes. For example, 1964 Republican presidential nominee Barry Goldwater presented a conservative message and sought to make inroads into the South. He had considerable success, even while Democratic incumbents continued to do well. As incumbents gradually retired and it became more respectable to vote for Republican House candidates, this divergence of voting results declined, resulting in a decline in split outcomes. During the realignment process, presidential results lead House results, creating a lengthy, but temporary, divergence of outcomes.

If realignment explains the presence of split outcomes, several important implications emerge. It suggests that the presence of split outcomes should rise and fall because realignment eventually brings convergence in the partisan vote for both offices. It also suggests that as realignment proceeds, any divergence between presidential and House results should be selective (not general), or in those districts where the presidential candidate is changing voting patterns. Finally, and perhaps most importantly this process reflects the fact that parties matter and that voters are making choices based on what parties represent. Incumbency has not displaced parties as the factor that shapes voting. The presence of incumbents slows down the conversion of an area to a different party, but this slowdown is only temporary and not a reflection of some general decline in partisan attachments (Brady et al., 2004).

The Evidence for Candidate-Centered and Realignment Explanations

With these alternative patterns of change as possibilities, Table 5.3 presents the pattern of differences in voting for Democratic House and presidential candidates for the last 50 years of elections. The first assessment focuses on the expectations of the candidate-centered explanation of change. The numbers in the table represent the average vote differences between House Democratic candidates and the Democratic presidential candidates.[23] Differences are calculated only for races in which an

Table 5.3   Democratic House–Presidential Vote Divergences, 1952–2000

	Democratic Presidential Candidate Percentage				
	0–29	30–39	40–59	60–69	70–100
Differences of House Democratic candidates (running versus Republican incumbents) from percentage of Democratic presidential candidates					
1950s	4	1	–4	–23	—
1960s	0	–2	–11	–17	–44
1970s	1	–3	–13	—	—
1980s	–6	–8	–9	–23	13
1990s	–3	–7	–10	–11	–
1992	2	–3	–5	0	—
1996	–3	–6	–9	–10	—
2000	–8	–13	–12	–29	—
Differences of House Democratic incumbents from Democratic presidential candidate percentages					
1950s	60	30	22	16	10
1960s	59	37	15	4	1
1970s	51	28	20	15	7
1980s	35	29	29	16	6
1990s	24	24	14	7	4
1992	22	23	16	3	5
1996	18	18	12	5	3
2000	32	30	15	10	5

Notes: Positive numbers indicate a Democratic House candidate ran ahead of the Democratic presidential candidate; negative numbers indicate a Democratic House candidate ran behind. Decades are grouped so that the apportionment is constant during the time period. The 1950s are 1952, 1956, and 1960; the 1960s are 1964 and 1968; the 1970s are 1972, 1976, and 1980; the 1980s are 1984 and 1988; and the 1990s are 1992, 1996, and 2000.

incumbent was present. Results are presented by whether a Republican or Democratic incumbent was present to indicate differences by party of the incumbent, in line with Figure 5.3 and Table 5.2. The results are grouped by the percentage of the vote received by Democratic presidential candidates, and calculated within decades to reduce the extent of data presented.

For the top half of the table, involving Democratic House incumbents, the Democrats should be able to run ahead of their party's presidential candidate where Democrats do the best (to the right), and they should have positive numbers on the right side. That is, their vote minus the presidential vote in that district should be a positive number because they can use the advantages of incumbency to run ahead of their presidential candidate within the district. In the bottom half of the table, when Democratic challengers are running against incumbent Republicans, the Republican incumbents should be able to hold the vote percentage of a Democratic candidate to less than that received by the Democratic presidential candidate. Numbers to the left should be negative for Democratic candidates, reflecting their running behind the presidential vote.

Given these expectations, the results turn out to be essentially the opposite of what would be expected if incumbents are able to move their vote away from the presidential vote. For Democratic candidates running versus Republican incumbents (the top half of the table), they do relatively better where Republican presidential candidates are weak, and they do worse where Democratic presidential candidates do better. That is, their differences are positive to the left (low Democratic presidential percentages) and negative to the right. For Democratic incumbents, the results are also the opposite of what we might expect. For the last five decades, Democratic incumbents run ahead of their presidential candidate in districts where the Republican presidential candidate did the best. To restate, Democratic incumbent candidates run relatively better than their presidential candidates in districts where their Democratic presidential candidate is weak.

Further, there is only a very modest pattern of differences becoming what we might expect if incumbents can push percentages away from the presidential vote. By the 1990s, Republican incumbents running where Democratic presidential candidates do poorly were able to hold Democratic candidates to percentages less than those received by their presidential candidate. That is, in the top half of Table 5.3, involving Republican incumbents in the 1990s, the numbers become increasingly negative to the left, indicating that they finally were able to run ahead of the vote for the Republican presidential candidate in that district. The differences are still very modest, however. Even while that occurs, however, the numbers to the right (for Democratic challengers running versus Republican incumbents in strong Democratic presidential districts) do not fit the pattern we would expect. Democratic challengers run further behind their presidential candidate in districts where the Democratic presidential candidate is strong.

The pattern for Democratic incumbents, in the bottom half of Table 5.3, is even more puzzling. Throughout the entire time period, Democratic candidates ran ahead of their presidential candidates by the largest amounts in districts where their presidential candidates do not do well. The pattern is the opposite of that suggested by Figure 5.3 and Table 5.2. Democratic House candidates ran ahead of their party's presidential candidates by the largest amounts where the Republican presidential candidates did the best, and they ran ahead by very modest amounts in districts where their presidential candidates did the best. The results are disconcerting if we are trying to find evidence that candidate-centered politics have emerged and that party incumbents are able to systematically move their vote away from that of their presidential candidates.

More important than the average percentage differences is the distribution of cases in which party incumbents were running. If incumbents were able to build on their party's presidential advantage in districts, we should find most of the cases of Republican incumbents to the left in Table 5.3 and most of the cases of Democratic incumbents to the right in Table 5.3. Table 5.4 presents the distribution by party of House incumbents who ran for reelection. In the 1950s, most Republican incumbents were running where their party's presidential candidate was strong. Then, in the 1960s, 69 Republican House incumbents found themselves running where the Democratic presidential candidate was very strong (i.e., where the Democratic vote was greater than 60 percent). Then in the 1970s through the 1990s, the pattern reverted to the expectation. The major change in 1952–2000 was experienced by

Table 5.4   Number of House Incumbents Running for Reelection by Democratic Presidential Results, 1950s–1990s

	Democratic Presidential Candidate Percentage				
	0–29	30–39	40–59	60–69	70–100
Number of Republican incumbents running for reelection					
1950s	47	240	205	3	0
1960s	18	82	163	63	6
1970s	71	181	169	0	0
1980s	46	169	98	2	1
1990s	36	210	304	8	0
Number of Democratic incumbents running for reelection					
1950s	6	57	425	126	59
1960s	46	48	175	110	79
1970s	54	157	405	57	51
1980s	10	106	310	36	36
1990s	8	50	344	78	97

Note: Decades are grouped so that the apportionment is constant during the time period.

Democrats. During the 1950s, most Democratic House incumbents were running where their presidential candidate was strong. Then, in the 1960s through the 1980s, a large number of Democratic incumbents were running in districts where their presidential candidate did not do well. By the 1990s, these numbers had declined significantly, although a substantial number remained.

The pattern does not fit what we would expect if candidate-centered politics were more pervasive and incumbents were able to build on the partisan inclinations of their districts. The distribution over time also indicates a declining number of cases in which incumbents have survived in situations where the opposing party's presidential candidate is winning.

What, then, might explain the patterns found here? The distributions fit the pattern we would expect if a gradual realignment is occurring, with presidential election results leading the way. Presidential candidates, Republicans in particular, were making inroads into areas held by House Democrats in the 1960s, 1970s, and 1980s. Nevertheless, Democratic incumbents survived as the transition occurred because they were well known. Democratic presidential candidates also were making inroads into areas dominated by Republican House incumbents. Even as they did, Republican House incumbents survived as the transition occurred. As shown next, once incumbents from each party were defeated or chose to retire, partisan transitions occurred, reducing the number of split outcomes.

This pattern in the presence of split outcomes is evident in Table 5.5, which presents the percentage of districts with split outcomes by Democratic presidential success. Split outcomes are consistently high in competitive districts, or those in which the Democratic presidential vote is between 40 and 59 percent. The interesting variation is in those districts where the Democratic vote for the president was less than 40 percent. In these districts, the presence of split outcomes was high in the 1960s through the 1980s, and then it declined in the 1990s.

The presence of more split outcomes was due to Republican presidential candidates making inroads into areas where Democratic House incumbents dominated, sometimes for several terms. The difference between the situation of incumbents in each party is perhaps more clearly evident in Figure 5.4. The figure presents the number of House Democratic and Republican incumbents running in districts that were won by the presidential candidate of the opposing party (not just 60 percent or more, but actually won by the presidential candidate). From the

Table 5.5 **Presence of Split Outcomes with Incumbents Present: Percentage of Districts with Split Outcomes by Democratic Presidential Results, 1950s–1990s**

	Democratic Presidential Candidate Percentage				
	0–29	30–39	40–59	60–69	70–100
Percentage of Districts with Split Outcomes: Incumbents Present					
1950s	13	14	38	1	0
1960s	45	22	40	22	7
1970s	40	42	39	2	0
1980s	16	34	56	5	0
1990s	14	18	31	2	0

Note: Results are grouped by decade so apportionment is constant during the decade.

Figure 5.4 **Number of Incumbents Running in Districts Won by Opposing Presidential Candidate, 1952–2000**

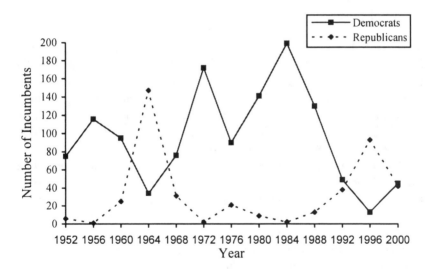

1950s through the 1980s, many, if not a majority, of Democratic House incumbents were running in districts won by a Republican presidential candidate. This situation declined dramatically in the 1990s.

The ability of Republican presidential candidates to make inroads into new districts created significant differences in the partisan vote between their vote and that for Democratic House incumbents, producing an increase in split outcomes. The ability of incumbents to survive in this situation is indicated by the following. In districts where a Republican presidential candidate received 60 percent or more of the vote and a Democratic incumbent was running, the percentage of elections producing split outcomes by decade was:

1950s: 76%
1960s: 58%
1970s: 94%
1980s: 85%
1990s: 74%

In contrast, only in 1964 and 1996 did a substantial number of Republican incumbents experience this situation.

The Dynamics of Realignment and Split Outcomes by Region

It is difficult to see these patterns as reflecting some generalized ability of incumbents to differentiate themselves from their party's presidential candidates. Instead of seeking to position themselves somewhat ahead of their candidate, many incumbents found themselves running where the other party's presidential candidate was winning the district as realignment unfolded. As the geographical bases of party success shifted, the presence of split outcomes rose and fell with it.

Realignment as a general phenomenon explains the rise and decline of split outcomes, but this has not played out in the same way in different regions of the country. Each evolution deserves a separate analysis. In the South, changes evolved steadily, with presidential results leading change. Outside the South, changes in electoral presidential and House election outcomes were more erratic over time, creating fluctuating occurrences of split outcomes from year to year.

The South

Electoral changes in the South have been profound (Black and Black, 2002), and the electoral bases have shifted significantly. The shifts in party electoral bases proceeded at different paces for presidential and House returns, creating a high level of split outcomes when the progressions were out of sequence (Buchler and Jarvis, 2004: 5). This transition had both a general and selective impact on the emergence of split outcomes in the South. At the general level, presidential results moved Republican before House results did. Because the average Democratic presidential result dipped below 50 percent, and the average Democratic House percent stayed well above 50 percent, there was a significant rise in split outcomes. Figure 5.5 presents the aggregate percentages over time, and indicates the differential pace of movement toward the Republican Party. As the two percentages converged in the 1990s, the percentage of split outcomes declined.

A selective movement by type of district also took place, reflecting the process of realignment. Republican presidential candidates began to do very well among affluent whites as early as the 1960s (Brewer and Stonecash, 2001). Despite this success, the Republican Party had not yet developed an organization, and there were no party candidates to take advantage of the vote for their presidential candidates. The Republican Party was able to offer challengers in urban and suburban districts, and as they did, split outcomes declined in these districts,

Figure 5.5   Progression of Democratic Decline by Office in the South, 1952–2000

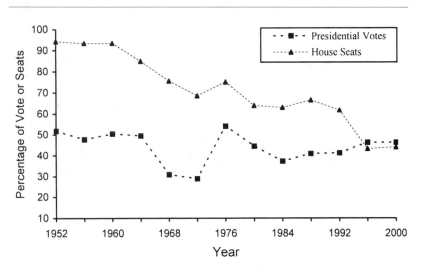

Source: Jerrold G. Rusk, *A Statistical History of the American Electorate* (Washington, D.C.: Congressional Quarterly Press, 2001), p. 140 (presidential vote percentages), p. 260 (percentage of House seats).

while remaining high through the 1980s in rural districts (Buchler and Jarvis, 2004: 10–13). Gradually, Republican House candidates in all types of districts realized the same level of success as their presidential candidates, creating similar alignments for both offices and reducing split outcomes.

Figure 5.6 indicates the differences and eventual convergence of Republican success for presidential and House candidates in the South by voter income level. In the 1952 through 1968 elections, Republican presidential candidates made significant inroads into more affluent districts, but House candidates did not, creating more split outcomes. In the 1972 election, volatility played a dominant role. McGovern was thoroughly rejected in the South, while many Republican candidates

Figure 5.6   Republican Success in Southern House Districts, by Income Levels, for Presidential and House Candidates, 1952–2000

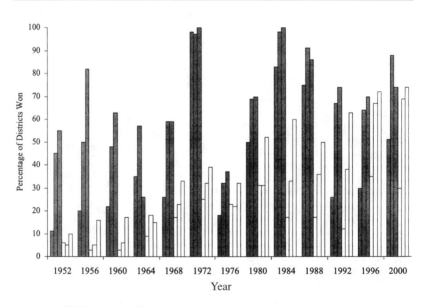

Source: US Bureau of the Census.

Notes: Dark bars represent Republican presidential candidate success rates (percent of each category of district won), and light bars are success rates for Republican House candidates (percent of each district category won). Districts are grouped from left to right within each election year by median family income within the district, with the lowest third presented first, then the middle third of districts, and the highest third of districts to the right within each year.

won seats. While House Republicans were gradually developing a base in more affluent districts, the surge to Nixon across all districts resulted in 66 percent of all districts being split. Carter's candidacy was well received in the South, creating similar party success by district income, and split outcomes occurred in only 24 percent of Southern districts. In the 1980 through 1988 elections, two matters were relevant. Republican presidential candidates again ran ahead of their House candidates in more affluent districts, and Mondale and Dukakis received the same reaction as McGovern in the South. This combination resulted in split outcomes in 34–56 percent of the districts. The Democratic Party responded to its eroding situation in the South by nominating Clinton and then Gore, both from the South. Their candidacies improved Democratic presidential success in the South and resulted in similar Republican presidential and House success levels by district income. By 1992–2000, Republican Party success rates by district income for House and presidential candidates were very similar, and the percentage of split outcomes dropped into the low twenties.

Three factors, then, created increases in split outcomes in the South over fifty years. First, Republican presidential candidates made inroads prior to the congressional wing. That produced consistently more split outcomes in more affluent districts. The same pattern prevailed in primarily white districts. One "wing" of the party was ahead of the other.

Second, there was also simple volatility, as the Democrats presented presidential candidates largely unacceptable within the South in 1972, 1984, and 1988. The rejection of these candidates produced increases in split outcomes.

Third, incumbency played a major role in affecting the pace of partisan change in House elections (Paulson, 2000: chapter 7). In many districts, the pattern was that Democrats held a House seat until an incumbent retired, and then a Republican won, and the seat stayed Republican after that, even as incumbent Republicans retired (Brady et al., 2004). Table 5.6 provides examples of the different patterns of change that occurred.[24] In some cases, such as Alabama 1, a conservative presidential candidate, such as Goldwater, coincided with the existence of an open seat in 1964. Without a Democratic incumbent present, a Republican won the House seat, and the only split outcome that occurred was in 1968, when Humphrey barely won a three-way race. Since then, the district has been uniformly Republican. In Louisiana 1, the Democratic presidential percentage fluctuated between 41 and 52

Table 5.6   Democratic Presidential and House Candidate Percentages, Incumbency, and the Occurrence of Split Outcomes in Selected Southern Districts, 1952–2000

	Alabama 1		Louisiana 1		Georgia 1		Mississippi 1		Alabama 5	
Year	P	H	P	H	P	H	P	H	P	H
1952	58	100	52	66	62	100	67	100	73	100
1956	51	100	**41**	**100**	58	78	73	100	65	100
1960	55	100	48	82	57	100	43	94	65	100
1964	27	40	**47**	**100**	40	**73**	**17**	**100**	**27**	**53**
1968	**21**	**38**	33	100	29	68	26	100	28	56
1972	24	18	**28**	**100**	25	**100**	**19**	**100**	**25**	**74**
1976	48	38	50	47	64	100	60	100	67	100
1980	41	0	46	0	55	100	55	63	54	94
1984	34	49	22	8	**41**	**82**	37	**88**	**40**	**96**
1988	37	40	29	6	**39**	**67**	40	**78**	**40**	**64**
1992	37	37	31	0	39	42	**42**	**59**	**41**	**66**
1996	39	34	37	0	45	32	42	31	**43**	**56**
2000	38	0	31	13	42	31	38	29	**43**	**99**

Source: Data compiled by the author.

Notes: P = presidential; H = House. Shaded cells refer to cases in which a Democratic incumbent was present. Bold numbers indicate a split outcome.

from 1952 to 1964. Three split outcomes occurred in Louisiana 1 because a Democratic House incumbent regularly prevailed. After 1972, the Democratic House incumbent retired, and after Carter's run helped to yield another set of Democratic victories, the district went Republican. In Georgia 1 and Mississippi 1, Democratic House incumbents hung on longer, while the district voted mostly for Republican presidential candidates, producing a relatively high number of split outcomes. In Georgia 1, the Democratic House incumbent retired in 1992 and Republicans took over. In Mississippi 1, a Democratic incumbent was defeated in 1994, converting the House district winner to the Republican column. Finally, Alabama 5 indicates how long change can take. The Republican presidential candidate won the district from 1984 through 2000, but an incumbent Democrat continued to win, producing a string of split outcomes. Electoral change is occurring, but incumbency slows down the emergence of uniform results within districts.

The presence of incumbents clearly contributed to the increase in split outcomes. The existence of incumbents slowed down partisan realignment, but it did not ultimately prevent it. Incumbents were able to temporarily create personal electoral bases within some districts that created partisan votes that were different from what the president was creating, but there was no general creation of divergent partisan voting patterns. Whatever candidate-centered voting that incumbents were able to create to ward off change, it was temporary, and partisan replacements gradually took place (Brady et al., 2004).

The Non-South

Outside the South, the sequence of change proceeded differently. The alignment of House districts was fairly well established by the early 1950s, unlike in the South. Figure 5.7 groups districts by the percentage of the non-South district population that is nonwhite by using census data. For each presidential election year, the percentage of districts won

Figure 5.7   Democratic Success in Non-South Districts, by Percentage Nonwhite, for Presidential and House Candidates, 1952–2000

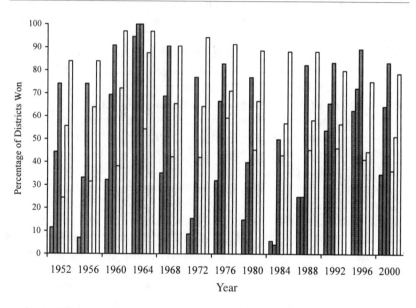

Source: US Bureau of the Census.

Notes: Dark bars represent Democratic presidential candidate success rates (percent of each category of district won), and light bars are success rates for Democratic House candidates (percent of each district category won). Districts are grouped from left to right within each presidential election year by whether the percent of the district that is nonwhite is less than 10 percent, 10–19 percent, or more than 20 percent.

by Democratic presidential candidates are grouped by whether they are low, moderate, or high in terms of the percentage of the district that is nonwhite.

As early as 1952, Democratic presidential and House candidates were able to win more districts that contained higher percentages of nonwhites. The crucial matter outside the South was the overall fluctuation of success for presidential candidates. As noted earlier, as realignment unfolded, each party was struggling with the direction it should take. In 1964, Republicans nominated a candidate who would be thoroughly rejected outside the South. The Democratic presidential candidate won almost all districts, while House results were more stable, producing an increase in split outcomes. In 1972, McGovern, the Democratic presidential candidate, was thoroughly rejected, again producing more split outcomes as House districts remained stable. In 1984 and 1988, Democratic presidential candidates again won few districts, increasing the presence of split outcomes. As was the case for the South, moderate Democratic candidates in 1992–2000 contributed to similar presidential and House results, and split outcomes declined.

The role of the instability of presidential results on split outcomes over the last 50 years is examined in Table 5.7. Columns 1 and 2 indicate the overall percentage of districts won by House and presidential candidates in each year. The percentage of House seats won by Democrats rises during the 1950s, and, except for 1964 and 1976, is relatively stable within the range of 41–49 percent of all seats. For presidential candidates, the stability of results is very different. The percentage of House districts won by Democratic presidential candidates varies all the way from 5 to 95.

This volatility produced major shifts in the partisan outcomes within districts. Columns 3 and 4 indicate the number of districts in which the presidency and House were won by both Republican candidates (R - R) and both Democratic candidates (D - D), respectively. Republicans dominated most districts in 1952–1960. In 1964, Johnson won by a large margin, shifting the bulk of districts (198) to D - D outcomes. Despite that, there were 110 districts outside the South where the Democratic presidential candidate won while the House Republican candidate won, creating a large number of split outcomes. In 1968, despite all the presumed turmoil, election outcomes returned to a more balanced distribution, and split outcomes declined. In 1972, 1980, and 1984, the Democratic presidential candidate lost almost all House districts, creating a large number of districts won by Democratic House

Table 5.7 Volatility of Presidential Outcomes and Split Outcomes, Non-South

| Year | Percentage of Districts Won by Democratic Candidates | | Uniform House–Presidential Party Outcomes | | Democratic Candidates Outcome | | | | |
	House (1)	Pres (2)	R - R (3)	Won H D - D (4)	Lost H Lost P (5)	Won P (6)	% split (7)	R^2 P (8)	R^2 H (9)
1952	28.1	15.6	208	63	44	5	15.4	.34	.19
1956	35.6	10.4	191	52	77	1	24.4	.36	.23
1960	42.6	37.0	139	109	47	28	23.0	.39	.22
1964	57.9	95.2	13	198	1	110	34.5	.39	.38
1968	44.8	39.0	137	116	43	26	21.4	.48	.36
1972	45.6	9.8	154	52	111	3	35.6	.53	.28
1976	61.1	37.5	99	121	85	15	31.3	.46	.23
1980	48.8	19.0	141	72	98	9	33.4	.49	.27
1984	47.1	5.3	136	46	129	1	41.7	.55	.30
1988	49.2	25.0	121	106	74	11	27.2	.56	.24
1992	49.7	58.0	82	153	24	45	22.7	.61	.34
1996	42.5	65.8	79	152	5	68	24.0	.61	.34
2000	41.6	45.2	110	134	24	36	19.7	.63	.33

Source: Data compiled by the author.
Notes: R^2 P and R^2 H, respectively, are the regression of presidential (P) and House (H) Democratic percentages on district scores for median family income, percentage urban, and percentage non-white. See text for an explanation.

candidates and the Republican presidential candidate. The elections of 1976 and 1988 created lesser versions of these situations. In 1992–2000, a higher number of districts had unified partisan outcomes, reducing the presence of split outcomes.

It is important to note what did not occur while all this volatility was occurring. The argument of the candidate-centered view of congressional elections is that candidates are increasingly able to separate themselves from presidential candidates. The changes that occurred over the last fifty years reflect two important matters. First, whereas House election results have been relatively stable or have changed gradually, presidential results have been more volatile. Overall, House incumbents have won fairly stable percentages of votes, and presidential candidate results have fluctuated around them. The presence of split outcomes is not due to incumbents increasing their vote percentages. Rather, it was the volatility of presidential results during the 1970s and

1980s that created more split outcomes. Incumbent members of Congress received relatively constant vote percentages and watched presidential results fluctuate around them.

Second, the candidate-centered view suggests that candidates should be able to separate themselves from the "deterministic" effect of district traits. A candidate who can establish a personal relationship should be bound less by the composition of a district. Whether a district is very affluent or has a high percentage of nonwhites should matter less over time in determining partisan votes. If candidates are creating unique constituencies, the demographics of districts should have less relevance as a means to predict variations in partisan vote percentages. One measure of this is the ability to predict statistically partisan voting by using the percentage of nonwhites, median family income, and the percentage of urban residents. The measure of this is the variance in partisan vote percentages explained (the R^2). This measure is presented in columns 8 and 9 of Table 5.7 and indicates how well these traits predict the Democratic vote across districts. The trend is that of a gradually greater association for both House and presidential percentages within districts. Even in the years of high split outcomes, R^2 was relatively stable. District composition has come to play a greater role over time. This reflects an underlying secular realignment, and not the emergence of candidate-centered politics. While this general stability has occurred, the level of presidential votes across districts has fluctuated, creating the rise and fall of split outcomes.[25]

In summary, the evidence on changes in split outcomes does not follow the pattern we would expect if candidates are able to diminish partisan voting behavior. Rather, the rise and fall of split outcomes reflects the consequences of realignment. As this realignment evolved, split outcomes first increased as presidential results changed. As presidential and House results have converged, the presence of split outcomes has declined.

6

The Rise and Decline of Split-Ticket Voting and Party Defections

Although the House district results provide valuable evidence on electoral trends, they do not reflect how individuals are voting, and ultimately our concern is with the partisan attachments of individual voters. For voters, the essential concern is what explains the trends in partisan attachments of the last fifty years. As indicated in Table 1.1 (Chapter 1), partisan attachments began to decline in the 1960s (Nie et al., 1976). Figure 6.1 presents three different ways in which that trend might be measured. The first is general ticket-splitting, or the percentage of all voters who vote for different party candidates in presidential and House elections. That percentage rose from 1952 through 1972.

This first measure reflects the behavior of all respondents in the NES surveys. During that time, the percentage of voters identifying themselves as independents when asked initially about their partisanship[26] began to increase. Because independents are more likely to split their tickets, the increase in ticket-splitting may be just a reflection of the increase in nonpartisans. The second measurement assesses the trend for ticket-splitting among only those who regard themselves as partisans, or the extent of ticket-splitting among those who identify as Democrat or Republican (not including leaners). The trend is essentially the same as for all ticket-splitters, but at a somewhat lower level. Finally, ticket-splitting understates the extent of defection by partisans

An earlier version of this chapter was presented at the 2002 Midwest Political Science Association Meetings, Chicago, Illinois, April 2002.

Figure 6.1   All and Partisan Ticket-Splitting, and All Partisan Defections, 1952–2000

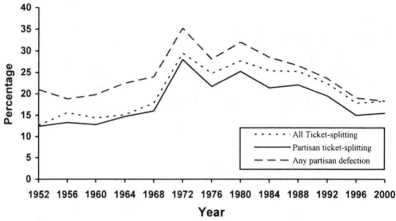

Source: NES Cumulative Data File, 1948–2002.

because it does not count those partisans who completely defect from the party. Some voters say they identify with one party, but then may vote for the other party's candidates for both the House and the president.[27] If all partisan defections (either a split ticket or complete defection) are included, the percentage is higher, but it follows the same pattern of an increase from 1952 to 1972, high levels during 1972–1980, and then a gradual decline. There is little ambiguity that partisan voting behavior decreased, and that it is now increasing (Bartels, 2000; Jacobson, 2000, 2003).

Explanations and Consequences

Again, there are two possible explanations of these trends, with each creating very different expectations of how change should proceed. The rise of partisan defections could reflect the emergence of candidate-centered politics. The economic issues that created the New Deal were presumably fading, and so the bases of partisan attachments were fading in relevance. House candidates in general were finding it easier to employ polling and direct mail to assess their situations and to respond with targeted messages. House incumbents were acquiring more office resources to build their name recognition and help constituents with problems—activities that would build goodwill among constituents and make it more difficult for a challenger to win. As House incumbents employed these resources, they were able to move voters away from straight-ticket voting, resulting in more ticket-splitting.

The contrasting argument is that realignment was occurring and that the transition created a decline and rise of partisan attachments. Each party contained considerable internal diversity in the 1950s, which grew during the 1960s and 1970s. Even as diversity was increasing, the issue of what role government should play was becoming more salient, and the parties were beginning to battle more about this issue.

Each of these arguments has very different implications for the trends that should prevail over time. The candidate-centered argument suggests that there should be no reversal of trends. With candidates having access to increasingly more resources (campaign funds and their benefits as well as the office resources of incumbents), candidates should be able to maintain and likely increase their ability to separate their vote from that for presidential candidates. How much of an increase is likely is not clear, but there certainly should be no decrease. Further, the increases in ticket-splitting and complete defections from a party should be general phenomena. That is, increases should be similar for those with differing beliefs about the role of government because the goal is to diminish the role of issues in organizing voting behavior. There also should be no pattern of ticket-splitting being a product of particular combinations of presidential and House candidates. If House Members are able to create unique identities, it should occur just as frequently for combinations of a Republican presidential candidate and a Democratic House candidate as for combinations of a Democratic presidential candidate and a Republican House candidate.

In contrast, a realignment perspective suggests that the trend will reverse and ticket-splitting should decline as the electorate sorts itself out between the two major parties. With the issue of the role of government remaining important, those voters who identify with a party but reject its issue positions will eventually respond by changing their partisan attachments. Those who were splitting their ticket because they disliked the party's positions will eventually become a smaller portion of each party. As the presence of dissenters within each party declines, ticket-splitting will decline overall and, more specifically, within each party's identifiers.

If realignment created the rise of ticket-splitting, then we should see it rise during the late 1960s and the 1970s. It was during that time period that Democrats enacted a significant number of prominent programs that expanded the role of government. These actions galvanized Republicans to begin advocating for a lesser role for government. The response of voters to changing party positions should not be expected to be rapid. Most voters do not follow politics closely nor do they study party positions closely (Patterson, 2002); voters generally do not have a lot of information about parties and issues (Macdonald et al., 2003). But voters do gradually and roughly discern shifts in party politics (Popkin, 1994), and they do gradually sort out differences between the parties (MacKuen et al., 2003). Further, even after recognizing that change is occurring, changing a partisan attachment is not an easy decision for voters. It still takes time for voters to be certain that a party has changed, and to conclude that a change is likely to be permanent. Some party candidates will draw attention to changes, whereas others are likely to blur distinctions. For all these reasons, changing party attachments takes time. Rather than changing a party identification, a more likely first step is for voters to engage in ticket-splitting. This practice should be most evident when transitions are occurring, and they should be most evident among those experiencing conflict between their views and the party.

If realignment is occurring, with Republican presidential candidates experiencing success attracting conservatives before many House candidates could, ticket-splitting initially should consist of voters choosing a Republican presidential candidate with a Democratic House candidate. Considering that the Republican Party has made its greatest advances in the South, this combination should be more prevalent there.

Increases in ticket-splitting should also be selective, with ideology playing a significant role. With each party acquiring more clarity as to its image, the greatest ticket-splitting should occur among those voters facing ideological conflicts between their own views and their current party attachments. Conservatives within the Democratic Party and liberals within the Republican Party should be the primary sources of ticket-splitting and of complete defections from their party identifications.

Finally, the presence of ticket-splitting should be accentuated by the presence of incumbents, who have greater visibility and who can continue to attract votes even as partisan realignment occurs. As the process of realignment evolves and incumbents eventually retire, ticket-splitting should decline. As realignment proceeds and incumbents retire, voters will be presented with open-seat matchups in which there is no pull of a highly visible local incumbent House Member. Eventually, those unhappy with their parties will move to another party, reducing conflicts and the need for ticket-splitting. Those voters experiencing inconsistency between their policy concerns and those of their parties will be able to reconcile their views with their party attachment and their votes, and ticket-splitting should decline.

If these patterns play out, what looked like a decline in partisan attachments during the 1970s, then, was not a movement away from parties, but an affirmation of the importance of parties to voters. Those who felt out of place with their party were not inclined to just accept that incongruity—they engaged in ticket-splitting until they changed their partisan attachment.

Assessing this realignment argument involves tracking the behavior of voters with differing beliefs over time. Because the first reaction of conflicted voters is likely to be ticket-splitting and not changing their party identification, this chapter focuses on ticket-splitting, and the next chapter examines changes in party attachments. The first concern is the extent to which ticket-splitting has reflected movement toward one party. Then the role of ideology and issues in creating ticket-splitting is examined, followed by an analysis of the impact of the spread of two-party competition and incumbency on ticket-splitting.

Nonpartisan Ticket-Splitting?

If voters were generally becoming less attached to parties, House candidates from either party should fare equally well in pulling voters away from straight-ticket voting. There should be just as many cases of voting for a Democratic presidential-Republican House candidate combination as there are cases of voting for a Republican presidential-Democratic House candidate combination. If, in contrast, ticket-splitting is driven by realignment, it should be most evident in situations in which presidential candidates (such as Republican candidates Nixon and Reagan) are trying to make in inroads into new constituencies, such as conservative voters in the South.

Figure 6.2 presents the overall level of straight-ticket voting for each party (Republican and Democratic presidential and House candidates) as well as the extent of split-ticket voting by the type of split that

Figure 6.2   Straight- and Split-Ticket Voting, 1952–2000

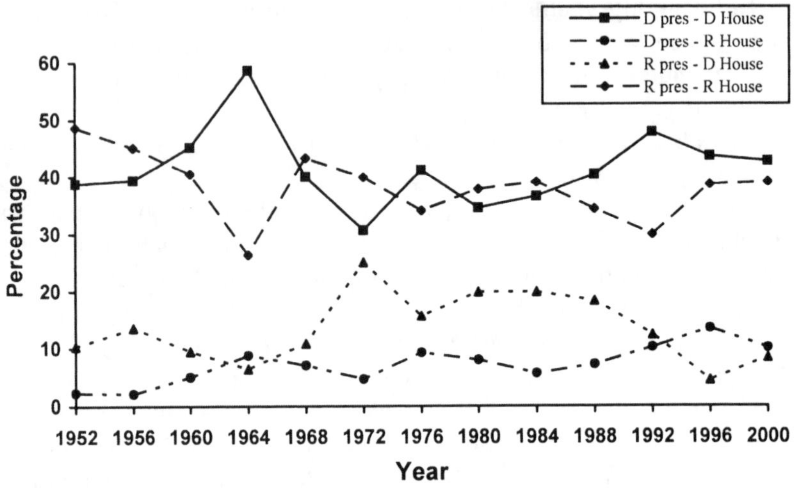

Source: NES Cumulative Data File, 1948–2002
Note: Only years with both presidential and House elections appear.

occurred. Each party experienced a roughly constant level of straight-ticket voting, with some fluctuations, from 1952 to 2000. The percentage of voters who voted for a Democratic presidential candidate and a Republican House candidate was modest and fairly low until 1992. The most common cases of split-ticket voting involved a vote for a Republican presidential candidate and a Democratic House candidate (called R - D situations hereafter).

Several matters are important about the trend of R - D situations. They rose during the late 1960s through the 1980s, when the transitions in party bases were occurring, and they then declined beginning in the 1990s, when there was considerable evidence that the electoral bases of the parties were sorting out by ideology, religion, and class. The prevalence of these vote splits is also greater in the South, as shown in Figure 6.3. Republican presidential candidates were able to win votes in this region, but the long history of voting Democratic in congressional elections, plus the numerous long-serving incumbents, created a relatively high level of split votes in that region. The rise in this behavior, however, was not confined to the South, suggesting there was a more general pattern occurring.

Figure 6.3   Split-Ticket Voting: Republican Presidential and Democratic House Candidates, 1952–2000

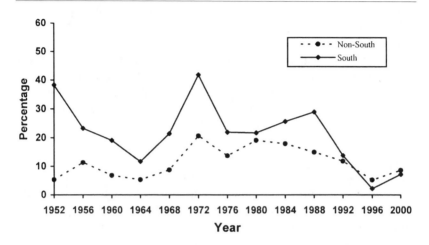

Source: NES Cumulative Data File, 1948–2002.
Note: Only years with both presidential and House elections appear.

The Role of Issues

If political realignment is gradually occurring, then we would also expect to see issues playing a significant role in creating ticket-splitting. Those concerned about an issue but currently in the "wrong" party should be most inclined to defect from "their" party. One of the most divisive issues shaping political change since the 1960s has been how much government should intrude into society to affect civil rights, housing, poverty, and educational opportunities. To track how issues have affected voting over time, we need surveys that ask about the same issues over extended periods of time. Our primary data source in this regard is again the National Election Study, which is conducted every two years. Very few questions about the role of government in the NES Cumulative Files were asked repeatedly over time. One recurring question in the NES files, however, involves the fundamental issue of the role of government. Since 1956, this question has been asked in one way or another: Should government should see to it that every person has a job and a good standard of living, or should individuals take care of these matters on their own?[28] Although it would be preferable to have a question that asks about the general role government should play in society, or to have responses to questions about other specific areas where government might be involved, this question is the only one asked that involved such a fundamental issue over an extended time period. Despite this limitation, this is a very valuable question.

When conservatives began to dominate the Republican Party, one of their primary concerns was that government was doing too much to undermine individual initiative and responsibility and not enough to encourage morality and pro-family policies. Their primary argument is that government actions should be devoted to supporting the private sector, because this is where new job growth should occur. Jobs created in the private sector generate additional societal wealth rather than consuming government revenues and requiring more taxes. From this perspective, it is important that government not play any role in providing jobs because that would encourage individuals to be less responsive to shifts in private markets. For many reasons, then, conservatives have become concerned about programs that would interfere with private markets. This concern should have increased in the 1960s following the enactment of numerous liberal programs that intruded into the private market in the areas of job training, welfare, and housing.

Table 6.1 presents the distribution of responses on the question of government or individual job responsibility for all respondents over time and by party from 1956 to 2000. Two trends are important. First, from 1956 to 1960, the responses indicate relatively broad support for the government playing a role in guaranteeing jobs. Among both Democrats and Republican identifiers, a majority of respondents were in support of government involvement, although Democrats were much more supportive.[29]

That consensus evaporated by 1964, and since then opinion has fluctuated from fairly evenly divided to much more supportive of relying on individual responsibility. Why this abrupt shift occurred is not clear. It could be that the enactment of a number of government programs with accompanying resources in the 1960s transformed the issue from an abstract one to a real one, and support for real government action was simply less than that in the abstract. Regardless, the abrupt transition created very different situations within each party. Among those identifying with the Republican Party, the shift was from a majority favoring government action to very strong support for individuals being responsible for their own situation. Although the transition seems large and abrupt, the timing roughly accords with when conservatives began to mobilize within the Republican Party (Rae, 1989; Brennan,

Table 6.1 Should Government or Individuals Be Responsible for Jobs? All Respondents and by Party, 1956–2000

| | All Respondents | | By Party Identification | | | | | |
| | | | Democrats | | Independents | | Republicans | |
Year	Govt.	Individ.	Govt.	Individ.	Govt.	Individ.	Govt.	Individ.
1956	57	27	63	22	50	28	48	34
1958	57	27	62	22	58	24	46	38
1960	60	24	66	19	64	20	49	33
1964	31	43	37	36	26	43	19	58
1968	31	47	39	39	26	64	21	55
1972	34	49	42	42	33	48	22	62
1974	31	49	39	39	30	52	17	66
1976	29	47	39	38	20	51	17	62
1978	21	54	29	45	22	54	9	71
1980	31	50	44	39	24	52	16	66
1982	31	52	40	41	29	50	17	72
1984	36	47	46	35	37	41	24	64
1986	31	59	41	49	33	56	18	74
1988	29	52	41	39	26	43	17	30
1990	37	46	47	37	34	37	25	62
1992	33	52	44	39	34	46	18	71
1994	35	56	48	41	39	44	20	75
1996	30	59	43	44	32	52	13	79
1998	39	45	51	33	40	40	24	65
2000	26	63	35	51	25	55	13	80
2002	21	47	32	29	22	46	11	63

Source: NES Cumulative Data File, 1948–2002.

Note: For this table, respondents were classified as supporting either government involvement or individual responsibility. The wording of the question about this has varied over time, so the coding to achieve this classification has varied over time as well. For the years 1956, 1958, 1960, 1964, and 1968, respondents were asked if they agreed or disagreed with the statement: "Should government guarantee jobs?" The introduction varied somewhat across time, and in some years respondents were asked if they strongly agreed or disagreed. All responses were collapsed into agree/disagree. Those who agreed were classified as supporting government involvement, and those who disagreed were classified as supporting individual responsibility. For the years beginning in 1972, respondents were presented with a seven-point scale and this language: "Some people feel that the government in Washington should see to it that every person has a job and a good standard of living. [1972–1978 and 1996 and later: Suppose these people are at one end of a scale, at point 1.] Others think the government should just let each person get ahead on their own. [1972–1978 and 1996: Suppose these people are at the other end, at point 7. And, of course, some other people have opinions somewhere in between, at points 2, 3, 4, 5, or 6.] Where would you place yourself on this scale, or haven't you thought much about this?" These responses were then recoded as 1 (for responses 1–3) and 2 (for responses 5–7). Those with response 4 were excluded. The wording of the question was changed in 2002.

1995; Hodgson, 1996). Among Democrats, the change was from a party fairly unified about the issue to one divided. That division has persisted since 1964.

The important matter is that the change altered the differences between the parties. The Republican Party became much more conservative on the issue, and very different from the Democratic Party. These differences may not have been immediately perceived by the electorate, but nevertheless, a difference emerged.

Issues and Party Defections

The erosion of a consensus about the role of government made it a more divisive issue. Republicans had never been strong supporters of government intrusion into the economy to help individuals, but this shift provided a basis for a sharper distinction between the parties. This difference between the parties became central to creating a realignment. With this issue becoming an ongoing source of contention between the parties, those who felt at odds with their party's stands should have been more inclined to split their tickets or completely defect from their party, while those in agreement should be strongly supportive of their party. Table 6.2 indicates how voters with different positions on the role of government voted in presidential and House elections. The results are grouped by decade to make it easier to see broad trends over the five decades involved. This focuses attention on broad trends in ticket-splitting and not on specific elections. Voters are divided by whether they think government should or should not be involved in jobs. Only partisans are examined in this table because these are the individuals who might experience a conflict between an existing party identification and their issue positions, which could in turn affect their vote choices.

Variations in support of the role of government have had a clear effect within each party on the extent of split-ticket voting. Democrats who supported a role for government presumably felt little cross-pressure, and over time approximately 80 percent of those holding this opinion continued to vote for Democratic presidential and House candidates (a straight party ticket). Indeed, the extent of straight-ticket voting among this set of voters has increased over time.

Those opposed to a government role regarding jobs, however, presumably felt considerable conflict, and their level of straight-party voting declined significantly in the 1970s and 1980s. By the 1990s, the effect of this issue appears to have subsided somewhat. Overall, those opposed to a government role were less supportive of Democratic candidates, but the difference was less during the 1990s. This could be because Bill Clinton sought more a moderate position on this issue

Table 6.2   Voter Choices by Party Identification, and Opinion on Government Role, 1950s–1990s

	Government should provide a job				Government should not provide a job			
Democrats	Voter Choices[a]				Voter Choices[a]			
Decade[b]	D - D	D - R	R - D	R - R	D - D	D - R	R - D	R - R
1950s	77.7	1.3	14.6	6.5	68.6	4.0	18.6	8.9
1960s	81.4	7.1	6.9	4.7	71.2	6.9	10.5	11.3
1970s	80.8	5.4	10.7	3.2	47.2	6.9	33.1	12.8
1980s	82.3	5.9	8.7	3.1	55.3	13.2	16.2	15.4
1990s	87.8	9.5	1.4	1.4	72.2	16.7	6.3	4.8
Republicans								
Decade[b]	D - D	D - R	R - D	R - R	D - D	D - R	R - D	R - R
1950s	4.1	.6	4.1	91.3	2.3	0	7.6	90.2
1960s	12.8	8.0	8.0	71.1	6.7	4.4	7.5	81.4
1970s	7.1	9.5	19.1	64.3	2.6	2.9	15.9	78.6
1980s	7.1	1.8	33.6	57.5	1.4	1.9	19.8	76.9
1990s	12.3	13.4	20.0	53.9	3.1	4.5	10.3	82.2

Source: NES Cumulative Data File, 1948–2002.

Notes: a. The first choice listed is that for president and the second is for the House candidate. D - D means a vote was cast for the Democratic presidential and House candidates, and D - R means a vote was cast for the Democratic presidential candidate and the Republican House candidate.

b. Results are aggregated within each decade. Decades are defined as: 1950s, 1952–1958; 1960s, 1960–1968; 1970s, 1970–1978; 1980s, 1980–1988; and 1990s, 1990–2000. Because the concern is the combination of presidential–House candidate choices, only years of presidential elections are included.

(Hale, 1995) or because the general polarization has pushed Democratic identifiers back into more loyal party voting.

For Republicans, the evolution of party support has also varied by voters' issue positions, and the consequences have increased with each decade. Those identifying as Republicans who were opposed to a government role have continued to vote at high levels for Republican presidential and House candidates.[30] Among those opposed to a government role, the percentage either completely defecting or splitting their ticket has increased with each decade.

Ticket-splitting, as we might expect, is greater among those experiencing conflict, or cross-pressuring. For both Democrats and

Republicans, those holding views about the role of government that conflict with their party's view are much more likely to defect completely or split their ticket. The levels of ticket-splitting by those in conflict are greater now than in the 1950s. For Democrats who support a government role, 15.9 percent voted a split-ticket in the 1950s, whereas 22.6 percent of those opposed to this role split their tickets; the difference by opinion was thus 6.7 percentage points. By the 1990s, the level of split-ticket voting for the former group was 10.9 percent, and 23.0 percent for the latter, a difference of 12.1 percentage points. For Republicans, the changes are more dramatic. In the 1950s, among those who were opposed to a government role, 7.6 percent split their tickets, whereas those who favored a government role split their tickets even less (4.7 percent), contrary to what we might expect. By the 1990s, 14.8 percent of Republicans in agreement with their party split their tickets, whereas 33.4 percent of Republicans supporting a government role split their tickets. For Republicans, the difference moved from those dissenting being less inclined to split by 2.9 percentage points to being more inclined by 18.6 percentage points. The difference would grow if all defections among Republican identifiers were included.

The same patterns play out in the South and in the remainder of the nation. In both areas, as shown in Table 6.3, defections among Democrats decline among those who support a government role, whereas they are much higher among those who do not think government should be involved. Republicans in both areas who think government should be involved with regard to jobs split their tickets and defected at high rates over time.

To summarize, the key question in reviewing these data is, Why did ticket-splitting and defections among those identifying with a party increase and then decrease? These trends can be explained by focusing on realignment and its effects. During the 1950s and early 1960s the two parties had modest differences on the issue of government involvement regarding jobs. During the 1960s, those identifying with the Republican Party shifted to a more conservative position on the issue. Those identifying with the Democratic Party became less supportive and remained more diverse in their views. The issue then became more salient and more of a source of political conflict, prompting those with views in opposition to their primary party position to split their tickets. That accounts for much of the increase in ticket-splitting.

The role of issues in the decline of ticket-splitting is more compli-

Table 6.3   Voter Choices by Party Identification, and Opinion on Government Role, by Region, 1950s–1990s

South	Government should provide a job				Government should not provide a job			
Democrats	Voter Choices[a]				Voter Choices[a]			
Decade[b]	D - D	D - R	R - D	R - R	D - D	D - R	R - D	R - R
1950s	74.7	0	17.6	7.7	64.5	3.2	29.0	3.3
1960s	81.6	2.7	10.9	4.7	66.7	1.0	17.7	14.7
1970s	78.2	2.3	14.9	4.6	40.8	4.9	49.5	4.9
1980s	83.1	2.4	12.9	1.6	57.8	14.7	14.7	12.8
1990s	90.6	6.3	3.1	0	60.0	23.5	5.9	10.6
Republicans	Voter Choices[a]				Voter Choices[a]			
Decade[b]	D - D	D - R	R - D	R - R	D - D	D - R	R - D	R - R
1950s	0	0	6.3	93.8	0	0	10.0	90.0
1960s	17.4	0	13.0	69.6	0	0	19.2	80.8
1970s	7.1	0	28.6	64.3	4.8	1.6	33.9	59.7
1980s	7.4	0	59.3	33.3	.9	0	27.9	71.2
1990s	13.3	13.3	33.3	40.0	2.3	6.8	9.8	81.2

Non-South	Government should provide a job				Government should not provide a job			
Democrats	Voter Choices[a]				Voter Choices[a]			
Decade[b]	D - D	D - R	R - D	R - R	D - D	D - R	R - D	R - R
1950s	78.9	1.8	13.3	6.0	69.9	4.3	15.1	10.8
1960s	81.3	8.7	5.4	4.6	72.8	9.1	8.0	10.1
1970s	81.7	6.6	9.1	2.6	50.5	7.9	24.8	16.8
1980s	82.0	7.5	6.8	3.8	54.0	12.5	17.0	16.5
1990s	86.8	10.6	.7	1.8	76.4	14.4	6.4	2.8
Republicans	Voter Choices[a]				Voter Choices[a]			
Decade[b]	D - D	D - R	R - D	R - R	D - D	D - R	R - D	R - R
1950s	4.5	.6	3.9	91.0	2.4	0	7.3	90.2
1960s	12.2	9.2	7.3	71.3	7.2	4.7	6.6	81.4
1970s	7.1	11.4	17.1	64.3	2.2	3.1	12.5	82.2
1980s	7.0	2.3	25.6	65.1	1.5	2.4	17.9	78.3
1990s	12.0	14.0	16.0	58.0	3.3	3.8	10.4	82.5

Source: NES Cumulative Data File, 1948–2002.

Notes: a. The first choice listed is that for president and the second is for the House candidate. D - D means a vote was cast for the Democratic presidential and House candidates, and D - R means a vote was cast for the Democratic presidential candidate and the Republican House candidate.

b. Results are aggregated within each decade. Decades are defined as: 1950s, 1952–1958; 1960s, 1960–1968; 1970s, 1970–1978; 1980s, 1980–1988; and 1990s, 1990–2000. Because the concern is the combination of presidential–House candidate choices, only years of presidential elections are included.

cated. Decline did not occur just because the electorate sorted itself out, such that there were fewer dissenters within each party. That sorting process is important and is the focus of the next chapter. As realignment proceeds, however, a crucial matter is the set of political candidates presented to voters. As the parties emphasize particular policies and the party image changes gradually, incumbents do not just move off stage as this evolution occurs. Many remain in office and affect the set of choices voters have and the ability of voters to act on their views. The role of incumbents and changing party competition help explain the pattern of declining defections.

Party Competition and Incumbency

As realignment unfolds, those who hold opinions at odds with their party, yet continue to identify with it, can resolve the conflict by voting for candidates of the other party. For voters to be able to defect, they need to be presented with candidates of the other party. Two matters can significantly constrain their ability to do that. First, one party may dominate an area so much that the other party does not present House candidates. Second, voters may be faced with a much more visible incumbent from their party and a challenger from the opposing party who has limited prospects for winning. The former prevents the possibility of even splitting a ticket (Burden and Kimball, 2002: 68), whereas the latter may inhibit ticket-splitting among those inclined to do so. There has been considerable change over time in both of these situations, which has brought about a decline in the extent of split-ticket voting.

First, there has been a significant change in the occurrence of uncontested House contests. Despite all the discussion of declining competition in House elections, the most significant change in recent decades has been a significant decline in the number of uncontested races (Stonecash, 2003a, 2003b). As Figure 6.4 indicates, two significant changes have occurred. In the South—the region undergoing the greatest change—the number of uncontested incumbents has steadily declined since the 1950s. In particular, both in the South and outside the South, a significant and marked drop occurred in the number of uncontested incumbents during the 1992–2000 elections.

To start with the most recent era, during 1992–2000 (as shown in Figures 6.1–6.3), a major drop in split-ticket voting occurred in both areas of the country. Those were also the first years in the past half century when a high percentage of voters were presented with both a

Figure 6.4 Number of Incumbents Uncontested, Presidential Election Years, by Region, 1952–2000

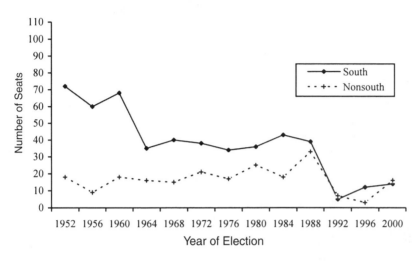

Source: Data compiled by the author.

Republican and Democratic candidate in House contests involving incumbents. That alone could have reduced the extent of ticket-splitting. Without that competition, many voters who identified with one party may not have been presented with a choice from their party. Republicans in the South may have been faced only with Democratic candidates. Their choices would then be to abstain in the House race or vote for a Democrat.

The other factor affecting voting is the presence of incumbents over time. Incumbents are invariably better known and better financed. Almost all incumbents (except in races targeted by the party committees) are more visible than their challengers. The presence of a well-known incumbent and a challenger who finds it difficult to create a presence and establish perceived policy differences is likely to constrain the extent of ticket-splitting.

The important matter is how voters with differing party identifications and views about government have reacted to incumbency situations, and how the situations they faced have changed.[31] Table 6.4 presents the situation for voters from 1976–2000. The top part of the table presents Democratic identifiers, sorted by whether they think government should or should not play a role in guaranteeing jobs. Several patterns are important. As noted earlier, Democrats who support a govern-

Table 6.4　Voter Choices by Party Identification, Opinion on Government Role, and Presence of an Incumbent, 1976–2000

	Presidential–House Candidate Vote Choices[a]			
	D - D	D - R	R - D	R - R
Democratic Identifier: government should provide jobs				
Republican incumbent	66.1	24.9	2.1	6.9
Democrat incumbent	90.6	1.6	6.6	1.2
Open seat	85.7	8.2	3.1	3.1
Democratic Identifier: government should not provide jobs				
Republican incumbent	42.5	35.8	3.3	18.3
Democrat incumbent	74.4	3.8	16.1	5.7
Open seat	64.7	14.1	12.9	8.2
Republican Identifier: government should provide jobs				
Republican incumbent	3.8	17.5	2.5	76.3
Democrat incumbent	13.2	2.6	44.7	39.5
Open seat	5.6	0	33.3	61.1
Republican Identifier: government should not provide jobs				
Republican incumbent	0.1	5.4	1.9	91.9
Democrat incumbent	3.7	1.3	32.8	62.3
Open seat	3.6	2.2	5.8	88.5

Source: NES Cumulative Data File, 1948–2002.

Notes: Percentages sum across columns to 100 for each incumbent situation; some rounding effects may be present.

a. Choice for the presidential candidate is always listed first: D - D means the voter chose the Democratic presidential candidate and the Democratic House candidate. D - R means a Democratic presidential candidate and a Republican House candidate.

ment role are more likely to vote a straight ticket. For each candidate situation, a Democratic Party identifier who supports a government role defects less often. The most important matter is how a Democrat behaves when presented with a Republican incumbent. A Democrat who supports a government role but is presented with a Republican incumbent is much more likely to vote for a Democratic presidential candidate, but a Republican House incumbent. Of the Democrats presented with this situation, 24.9 percent split their votes in this way. Incumbents do have an advantage, and their presence pulls voters away from their normal partisanship. For Democrats who do not support a role for government, the defections are even greater when presented with a Republican incumbent, with 35.8 percent voting for a Democratic presidential candidate and a Republican House incumbent.

　The same pattern prevails for Republicans. Republicans who

oppose a government role are less likely to defect for each candidate situation. However, those who oppose government involvement, but are presented with a Democratic House incumbent, are more likely to split their ticket by voting for a Republican presidential candidate and a Democratic House candidate. The defection rate for Republicans is the greatest for those who support government involvement and are presented with a Democratic incumbent. For both Democratic and Republican Party identifiers, the presence of open-seat contests produces much lower rates of defection.

The finding that incumbents pull people away from voting for candidates from their parties is not new and it is not surprising. To some, it might be seen as confirming the candidate-centered view. The concern here, however, is with the choices presented to voters and how the candidate choices presented to voters have changed over time. Table 6.5 summarizes the incumbent situations presented to voters for 1976–2000 by areas of the nation. Outside the South from 1976 to 1992, the situation was that approximately 50 percent of voters were presented with a Democratic incumbent and between 30 and 36 percent of voters were presented with a Republican incumbent. Most incumbents were contested, but Democrats dominated. In the South, the dominance of Democratic incumbents for 1976–1988 was even greater, with many Democratic incumbents running unopposed.

The political choices presented to voters changed in the 1990s. Prior to 1992 in the South, voters were considerably more likely to be presented with Democratic than Republican incumbents. Beginning in 1992, the incumbent-party choices became much more balanced. In the South in 1992, the percentage of open-seat contests increased significantly. In 1996 and 2000, voters were presented with more Republican incumbents and fewer Democratic incumbents, and the percentage of contests with Republican incumbents also increased significantly.

The change that occurred in 1992 suggests it may be useful to break situations into pre-1992 and 1992–2000, and compare the different situations voters faced. Table 6.6 groups voters by their party identification and views about the role of government, and compares the voting choices they faced for different time periods. Comparing Democratic identifiers first, the major change these voters faced, regardless of their opinions, was in an increase in the percentage of open seat contests in the 1990s. There was also an increase in the percentage of voters presented with Republican incumbents, such that their ticket-splitting would increase.

The changes in choices experienced by Republican Party identi-

Table 6.5   Distribution of Political Choices Presented to Voters, by Region and Year, Presidential Elections, 1976–2000

	Incumbent Present and Party				
	Candidate Choices Presented to Voters[a]				
	Republican Incumbent		Democratic Incumbent		
South	R - No D	R - D	No R - D	R - D	Open seat
1976	1	18	14	53	14
1980	0	23	35	37	5
1984	0	19	23	48	10
1988	2	16	41	35	6
1992	2	10	0	49	39
1996	6	52	1	26	14
2000	19	37	9	25	9
Non-South	R - No D	R - D	No R - D	R - D	Open seat
1976	2.7	29.0	5.1	48.6	14.7
1980	1.4	35.5	6.5	48.8	7.9
1984	3.1	27.6	7.2	55.1	7.0
1988	10.9	26.4	8.1	48.4	6.1
1992	1.0	28.6	4.2	51.1	15.0
1996	2.2	48.0	1.0	40.7	8.2
2000	1.9	42.5	5.3	40.5	9.9

Source: NES Cumulative Data File, 1948–2002. Classification of situations respondents faced was derived from vcf0902 and vcf0903.

Notes: Percentages sum across columns to 100 for each year; some rounding effects may be present.

a. R - D refers to whether a Republican or Democratic candidate was present. Whether the candidate was an incumbent is designated at the top of the columns. No R or No D means that no candidate from the party was present.

fiers, however, are very different. For 1976–1988, a majority of all Republican identifiers were presented with Democratic incumbents. Those Republicans who were opposed to a government role were faced with more Democratic than Republican incumbents. By 1992–2000, a significant change had occurred. Half of all Republican identifiers were presented with Republican incumbents, and 51.7 percent of those opposed to a government role (the bulk of the party) were presented with a Republican incumbent. In the 1990s, those who were strongly inclined to support the Republican Party were presented with fewer situations in which a Democratic incumbent was present.

Realignment affects voters by changing the choices presented to

Table 6.6   Incumbency Situations Faced by Party Identifiers, and Opinion on Government Role, 1976–1988 and 1992–2000

Party ID	1976–1988 Incumbent Present			1992–2000 Incumbent Present		
	Rep.	Dem.	Open	Rep.	Dem.	Open
Democrat						
All	23.3	68.5	8.2	32.7	52.7	14.6
Should	19.8	71.8	8.4	25.9	55.3	18.9
Should not	26.4	64.3	9.3	37.6	51.0	11.5
Republican						
All	39.8	50.6	9.6	50.0	36.6	13.3
Should	35.1	59.0	6.0	30.6	45.6	23.8
Should not	40.9	49.0	10.2	51.7	35.7	12.6

Source: NES Cumulative Data File, 1948–2002.

Note: Percentages sum to 100 across categories for each time period; some rounding effects may be present. For example, for all Democratic identifiers during 1976–1988, 23.3 percent faced a Republican incumbent and 68.5 percent faced a Democratic incumbent.

them. Areas that were once dominated by one party began to experience two-party competition and the presence of incumbents from the previously minority party. This change was most obvious in the South, with the Republican Party making inroads beginning in the late 1980s. That changed the choices presented to party identifiers and put fewer voters in situations where incumbents from the opposing party were present. These changes helped bring down the level of ticket-splitting.

Summary

The rise of split-ticket voting is generally portrayed as an indicator of electoral disengagement from the parties. That is, it is presented as if it involves rejection of parties in general and not a single party. The argument of this analysis is that the rise and decline of split-ticket voting is more of a defection from a party based on issue conflict. The long-term resolution is different for each party. For Democrats, it appears that tension over the issue of the role of government is now less than it was during the 1980s. The division within the party over this issue is still there, but the impact of the difference of opinion is now less than it was. For Republicans, the impact of differences of opinion over this issue is still significant, but those who support the nonmajority opinion are now a dwindling percentage of all Republicans.

The most important matter is what the rise and decline of split-ticket voting represents. It is not a rejection of parties, per se, but of a specific party due to the conflict the party identifier has about an issue position of the party. That conflict leads to a short-term resolution that involves reduced support for the party's candidates. In the long-term, we expect that voters are likely to change the party they support. The analysis of the evolution of that process follows.

7

Changes in Party Identification

Voters who have a conflict between their issue concerns and party identification can cope by splitting their tickets—voting selectively for some of "their" party candidates and for some candidates of the other major party. Although this practice may suffice in the short run for those experiencing such conflicts, eventually a voter is likely to think about changing party identification. If a long-term sorting out of the electorate is occurring, with issues playing a significant role in reshaping party loyalties, then we should see shifts in who identifies with which party.

These shifts in party identification actually are occurring; the important matter is how this may affect the overall level of partisan identification. In the last 30 to 40 years, one of the most widely discussed trends has been the general decline in partisan identification. Figure 7.1 presents trends in the percentage of independents from 1952 to 2002, based on NES surveys. People were asked two questions. First: "Generally speaking, do you usually think of yourself as a Republican, a Democrat, an independent, or what?" Respondents who do not choose a party are then asked: "Do you think of yourself as closer to the Republican or Democratic Party?" Those who do not choose a party in response to the initial question are regarded as independents. Those who do not lean toward either party in response to the second question are regarded as "pure" independents, or those who do not identify with a party at all.

An earlier version of this chapter was presented at the 2004 Midwest Political Science Association Meetings, Chicago, Illinois, April 2004.

Figure 7.1   The Rise of Independents, 1952–2002

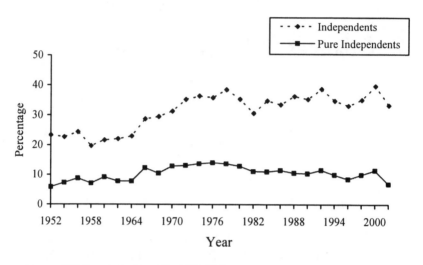

Source: NES Cumulative Data File, 1948–2002.

In the last 50 years, the percentage of voters who regard themselves as independent has increased. Beginning with the 1966 election, the percentage of both independents and pure independents increased substantially. Independents increased from roughly 25 to 40 percent, and pure independents increased from about 8 to 13 percent. After these increases in the mid-1960s, both categories have remained at relatively constant levels.

Table 7.1 provides more detail on these changes and indicates why so many have concluded that there is a movement away from partisan identification among voters. The table groups all NES respondents by decade, and reports the percentage within each decade who responded that they are Democrats or Republicans, and the percentage of those who indicated they lean toward either party. The percentage that resists being seen as partisan, even when asked if they lean toward a party, is shown in the middle column as "independent." Over time, there has been a decline in the percentage indicating they are partisan (choosing either party), with almost all the change coming from a decline in identification with the Democratic Party. The most important change has been the rise in the percentage indicating that they do not initially identify with a party but lean to a party. In the past 50 years, there has been

Table 7.1   Party Identification Changes, 1950s–2000s

	Democrat	Lean Dem.	Independent	Lean Rep.	Republican
All Respondents					
1950s	48.1	7.8	7.2	6.7	29.8
1960s	48.9	8.2	9.5	6.8	26.3
1970s	40.5	12.0	13.5	9.3	23.3
1980s	39.3	14.0	11.4	12.8	27.0
1990s	36.2	13.5	10.1	11.4	28.6
2000s	34.5	14.4	9.2	13.0	28.6
Change, 1950s to 2000s	−13.6	6.6	2.0	6.3	−1.2

Source: NES Cumulative Data File, 1948–2002, all years.

a net increase of 12.9 percentage points in this category. Indeed, since the 1980s the percentages in this category for both parties were considerably higher than in prior decades. It is understandable why some would see a decline in partisan attachments.

The Argument

The first issue to be explained is why the percentage of self-defined independents and pure independents (excluding leaners) would increase if realignment is occurring. This increase was widely interpreted as dealignment, or as reflecting a general decline in attachment to parties within the electorate. Then there is the issue of why there would be a decrease in the percentage of pure independents. This decline is a puzzling change if candidate-centered politics is flourishing. If a long-term realignment is occurring, how does this approach explain an increase in independents and then a decrease in the percentage of pure independents?

The arguments of this analysis are twofold. First, the rise in self-defined independents does not reflect the decline in partisanship that is generally presumed. Second, the focus on the aggregate percentage of independents has led to a neglect of the disaggregated shifts in party identification responses associated with realignment. Although the overall increase in independents is interesting, the more revealing changes are those associated with differing views of voters. These shifts and the rise of independents reflect the process of transition as secular realignment occurs.

Are Independents Nonpartisan?

Before exploring the second argument, which is central to this analysis, the meaning of an increase of self-identified independents for partisanship needs to be examined. This increase was generally seen as reflecting a growing disengagement from partisan behavior within the electorate. The simple and plausible presumption was that those not identifying with a party were also less likely to engage in partisan behavior. That presumption has been carefully examined and found not to be the case.

As noted, those who initially define themselves as independent can be broken down into those leaning toward a party and those who are pure independents. Because most of the increase has come in the category of those who lean toward a party, the important matter is how these leaners actually behave. Keith et al. (1992) assessed the reported voting behavior of leaners compared to strong and weak partisans and found that leaning partisans act just like weak partisans.

Table 7.2 extrapolates Keith et al.'s (1992) information through the 2002 elections. The left column presents the partisan identification responses of voters. The voting choices of each category of response are then presented by decade. The numbers are the percentages of those in each category voting for their party's candidates for president and the House and then the percentage voting a straight ticket, or for both candidates of their party. The important matter is whether those who lean toward a party are very different from those who are strong or weak partisans. As the results indicate, those who say they lean toward a party have partisan records similar to those who say they are weak partisans. The evidence supporting the arguments of Keith et al. is strong. Leaners are very much like weak partisans, and the presumption that the rise of independents who lean to a party reflects disengagement from parties is not persuasive.

Cohort Changes over Time and Alternative Expectations

Even though leaning partisans do not reflect diminished partisanship, there has been an increase over time in the percentage of those not inclined to identify as partisans. This leads to the question of who is changing. One approach to this question is to focus on how cohorts have changed. The two broad interpretations of trends in partisanship

Table 7.2 Partisan Voting by Party Identification Response, 1950s–1990s

	Decade														
	1950s			1960s			1970s			1980s			1990s		
	P	C	ST	P	C	ST	P	C	ST	P	C	ST	P	C	ST
Percentage of Democrats Voting Democratic															
Strong D	84	93	84	90	91	87	81	91	77	89	88	82	95	89	88
Weak D	63	82	60	70	80	68	59	79	52	66	73	56	78	77	70
Lean D	63	72	60	74	73	66	66	79	58	72	79	67	72	74	69
Percentage of Republicans Voting Republican															
Lean R	93	82	80	81	78	75	85	71	65	86	64	59	69	72	66
Weak R	93	89	88	73	74	65	85	74	67	88	70	66	70	74	66
Strong R	99	95	95	95	93	90	97	85	84	96	80	80	92	87	88

Source: NES Cumulative Data File, 1948–2002, all years.

Note: Results are aggregated within each decade. Decades are defined as: 1950s, 1952–1958; 1960s, 1960–1968; 1970s, 1970–1978; 1980s, 1980–1988; and 1990s, 1990–2002. Because the concern is the combination of presidential–House candidate choices, only years of presidential elections are included. P = percentage voting for their party's presidential candidate, C = percentage voting for their party's House candidate, ST = percentage voting for party's presidential and congressional candidates.

again provide contrasting expectations of how different age groups should behave.

The decline-of-party, candidate-centered interpretation suggests there should be a general increase in the presence of independents across all age cohorts. An increase in independents might be greater in the generation coming of political age when parties have come to mean less, but the candidate-centered phenomenon affects the entire society, so all voters should become less partisan over time.

In contrast, a realignment perspective suggests that although there should be cohort differences, there should also be a general decline over time in identification as an independent. Cohort differences in independent identification should occur for those coming to political awareness when party differences were diminished. As reviewed earlier, the differences between the two parties were pronounced during the 1930s and 1940s, when Democrats supported a much greater role for government. Those born before the 1930s would see a clear difference between the parties. Those born between 1930 and 1950 would see less of a difference because the internal diversity of the parties became more evident. Those born after 1950 would be coming to political awareness during the 1970s, when the voting differences between the parties in

Congress were beginning to decline and each party presented very diverse members to the electorate. Those born in 1950 and after should initially be less inclined to see a difference between the parties and more inclined to identify themselves as independent. As the older generation dies off and the post-1950 cohort replaces them in the electoral pool, the replacement would gradually increase the percentage of all respondents who identify themselves as independents.[32]

The crucial difference in expectations involves what should prevail after the 1970s for each cohort if realignment is occurring. If the electorate did not see a difference between the parties during the 1960s and the 1970s, but differences became more apparent during the 1980s and 1990s, then we should expect to see a gradual decline in the percentage of independents within each cohort. The youngest cohort, which did not initially see a difference, should decline the most as differences become clearer to them.

Figure 7.2 presents the percentage of independents (in response to the initial question) within each age cohort over time. That is, each line tracks the responses of those born during particular years for subsequent years. Several patterns are important. First, the voters in each successive cohort were more likely to regard themselves as independents.

Figure 7.2   Percentage of Independents by Age Cohorts, 1952–2002

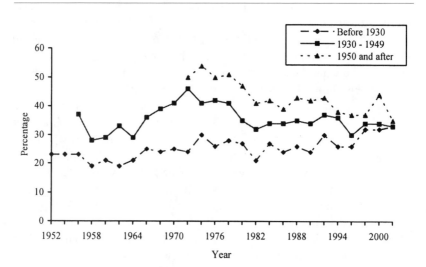

Source: NES Cumulative Data File, 1948–2002.

During the 1970s, 50 percent of those born in 1950 and after defined themselves as independents, 40 percent of those born from 1930 to 1949 defined themselves as independent, and approximately 25 percent of the oldest cohort defined themselves that way.

Second, the increases for the pre-1930 and 1930–1949 cohorts are relatively modest during the 1970s. The oldest cohort increases by somewhat less than 10 percentage points and the middle cohort increases by about 10 percentage points. The probable sources of those increases are discussed below.

Third, and most important, is what has transpired since the 1970s. If candidates are able to move voters away from partisan attachments, the increase in independents that occurred during the 1970s should persist, and perhaps increase, in subsequent years. There should be no decline in the presence of independents among all cohorts. If realignment is occurring, we should see a gradual decline in independents as voters sort themselves out between the parties. As Figure 7.2 indicates, those in the two most recent cohorts show a gradual decline since the 1970s in the percentage who regard themselves as independent. They are gradually choosing to identify with one of the two major parties. The only cohort that does not fit the pattern involves those born before 1930. This group shows a very gradual increase in the presence of independents, but much of that increase came in 1992–2000, well after the emergence of candidate-centered politics.[33]

To summarize the evidence, it is clear that the overall percentage of independents has increased. The bulk of this movement involves voters identifying themselves as leaning to a party, but there is no evidence that those moving into the leaning category are less partisan in their voting. That increase does not reflect a decline in partisan behavior. The rise also coincides with what we would expect if many voters just entering the political process were unclear about the extent of differences between the parties. The declines in the presence of independents (except among those born prior to 1930) also fits with what we would expect if voters are perceiving differences between the parties and sorting themselves out between the parties.

Disaggregating Changes in Independents: The Role of Realignment

Although these analyses suggest that realignment might be occurring, they do not address the fundamental issue of whether individuals might change their party identification over time. The essence of the secular realignment argument is that voters gradually respond to evolving party alternatives and change their party identifications. If issues create realignment of party identification, those voters who feel "out of place" should gradually change their party identification. Specifically, do those who have an issue conflict with their party change, and, if so, how might this create an impression of disengagement from parties?

Even though voters may eventually change their partisan identification, that process is not likely to be easy and abrupt. From what we know, very few voters suddenly switch from one party to another. As explained in the next section, that process is likely to be lengthy and incremental. That process, as party bases and images change, creates transitions in the attachments of voters. Those transitions are selective, with conservatives gradually moving toward the Republican Party and liberals gradually moving toward the Democratic Party. While these transitions are occurring, we expect to see an increase in independents. Only when the transition process culminates, if that ever occurs, should the percentage of independents significantly decline.

The Issue of Changes in Partisan Attachments

The argument of this analysis is that voters gradually assess the compatibility between their views and their party identifications, and when conflicts exist, party identification changes slowly. This is not a theoretical view that everyone has accepted. Theories about the basis of party attachments and their susceptibly to change over time have evolved considerably in the last 50 years. That evolution has not, however, produced a consensus about how much individuals are inclined to change their party identifications.

The background of this debate needs to be explained before moving to an analysis of the data. The statement that voters change their partisan attachments over time has generated considerable controversy. The essence of the dispute revolves around whether voters form affective (emotional) attachments to parties and find it difficult to change those attachments, or whether there is an ongoing cognitive assessment of party policy positions and an adjustment of partisan attachments when voters find their current party positions incompatible with their personal views. Those who adhere to the former interpretation see voter identification with a party as something that is formed early in life, is based on identification with a social group, is emotional, and is very unlikely to change over time. In this view, voters do not follow party positions much and do not continually adjust partisan attachments to ensure compatibility of personal views with party positions. The alternative view sees much more possibility of voter cognition of the political world and adjustment as party positions change (Abramowitz and Saunders, 2004).

Both views allow for aggregate change, but the interpretation of how it occurs differs. For those stressing an affective basis of attachments, it is likely that families pass along partisan attachments through extensive positive and negative commentary about various social groups and where the family "belongs." This gradual transmission (and stability) of partisan attachment is apparently disrupted only in eras when intense political events occur and party images are sharply defined (such as for Democrats and Republicans during the Great Depression and the early years of the Franklin Roosevelt administration). When such events create a confrontation over a major issue, such as the role of the national government, a new cohort may change its overall distribution of attachments from those prevailing, resulting in an aggregate change. Change in this view is largely a product of occasional major events. In contrast, those who presume ongoing cognitive assessments see change as gradual and continual as voters assess party positions and make individual decisions about their loyalties.

The Party Identification Debate

Arbitrating between these competing arguments is obviously crucial to an analysis that seeks to explain how changes in partisan attachments occur over lengthy periods of time. In the modern era of survey analysis, the initial and dominant view of voters was presented in *The American Voter*, in which Campbell et al. (1960) describe party identification as a "psychological identification" or as a concept "to characterize the individual's affective orientation to an important group-object in his environment. Both reference-group theory and small-group studies of influence have converged upon the attracting or repelling quality of the group as the generalized dimension most critical in defining the individual-group relationship, and it is this dimension that we call identification" (p. 121).

This view, as articulated later by Green et al. (2002), is that voters identify with social groups, and these identifications with a group are fundamental and largely unchanging. These attachments affect the possibility for change to occur. "Partisan change among adults often has little to do with unfolding political and economic events" because of "the public's inattentiveness to politics" and because "partisans ignore or deflect information that is inconsistent with their party attachments" (pp. 6–7). The combination of powerful social identification, limited knowledge, and biased interpretation of existing evidence leads to very little change in partisan identifications within the electorate.

Although this view of voters as largely stable in their party identification seemed persuasive, there was a gradual emergence of a perspective that issues do matter, and, that if they do, incongruities between individual and party positions prompt some voters to change. During the 1970s and 1980s, numerous studies emerged arguing that issues affect partisan voting (Pomper, 1972; Black and Black, 1973; Jackson, 1975; Ladd and Hadley, 1975; Weatherford, 1978; Shively, 1980; Franklin and Jackson, 1983; Franklin, 1992), and suggesting that voters change their partisan attachments over time as new issues emerge or old ones become more salient. The argument that voters use issues to make assessments of which party they should support (e.g., a running tally) was made most forcefully by Fiorina (1981a). He suggested that voters were engaged in a fairly systematic retrospective assessment of how the parties were performing and that they adjusted their partisan attachments accordingly. As Fiorina summarized this view two decades later, scholars in the 1970s were witnessing change, and they were formulating analyses with that perspective in mind (Fiorina, 2002). Studies continued to appear that found that party identification changes were associated with ideology (Abramowitz, 1994; Abramowitz et al., 2002; Abramowitz and Saunders, 2004), race (Carmines and Stimson, 1989; Black and Black, 1987), religious attachment (Layman, 1999, 2001), and income (Stonecash, 2000).

The presumption that voters assess issues and change their partisan attachment in response to conflicts between their views and the positions of the parties has not gone without challenges. Green et al. (2002) argue that two kinds of evidence support the claim that partisan attachments are stable and change is limited. First, they present evidence that aggregate partisan identification distributions in the electorate are very stable over long periods of time (pp. 14–51). Second, they analyze panel studies, or surveys of the same individuals over time, and conclude that there was little change in partisan identification during the time spans involved. Further, whatever change is evident in these studies they attribute largely to measurement error. That is, what appears to be change is more of a reflection of the limited precision of survey questions (Green, 1991; Green and Palmquist, 1990; 1994).

Despite the efforts to restore the claim that individual voters do not change their partisanship over time, the arguments in support of this position have several flaws. First, the two conclusions—that voters assess change and respond versus a claim of partisan stability—present a false dichotomy that limits how we understand change. Second, some of the evidence for stability is based on aggregate data, which can conceal considerable individual-level change. Third, the analyses based on tracking the same individuals over time are based on fairly limited time spans. The interpretations of the results tend to emphasize the stability found, rather than to demonstrate that everyone is stable. These analyses also focus on the overall extent of stability and not whether those with particular views move in specific directions. Fourth, the argument that measurement error accounts for whatever change occurs, a technical issue, is not convincing.[34] Each of these first three matters deserves a brief comment here.

As is often the case in social science analyses, questions of whether A or B is true generate interesting and consuming debates, but they represent a false dichotomy. Both the argument about stability and that about change have considerable validity, and both can be accepted without excluding the other. Most voters develop a strong affective attachment to parties and are generally disinclined to reassess the political world regularly. These voters create considerable stability. Others engage in ongoing scrutiny and some change their partisan attachments. It is important to analyze this last group in order to understand change. The majority may be stable, but if a small segment of the electorate experiences conflict and gradually alters its partisan identification (MacKeun et al., 1989), and small segments keep doing this, the cumulative effect over an extended time period would be a secular realignment within the electorate (Key, 1959).[35]

To restate this, both stability among many and change among some may occur. To argue that voters (as if this encompasses all voters) behave in a particular way imposes a blanket uniformity on voter behavior that does little to help us understand incremental change. If there is slow but systematic and continual change among a small set of voters in their partisan attachments, then their changes may well be seen as an increase in disengagement from parties when it really represents the process of transition. The first problem, then, is an inappropriate framing of the issue.

The second problem is that some of the evidence for stability is aggregate in nature. That is, it involves the overall percentage of voters who are Democrats or Republicans. Although the extent of aggregate stability is interesting, it does not directly address individual behavior. Within aggregate stability, there could in fact be considerable change in the composition of the aggregate support for either party (Dreyer, 1973: 715). For example, 45 percent could support the Democratic Party in 1980 and 2000, but aside from death and new entrant changes, there could be considerable movement in and out of the party. Finding aggregate stability is certainly interesting, but it does nothing to establish that individuals are correspondingly stable.

The third problem involves the panel studies, or surveys that track the same people over time, but never cover more than four years. Several problems exist with the analysis of these panel studies. They cover a limited time period. If an individual is finding it difficult to abandon his or her existing party identification, four years may be far too short a time period for analyzing change. Even if the length of time could be accepted, the interpretation of panel studies leaves something to be desired. Most analyses find that a high percentage of voters (60–90 percent) retain the same party identification over four years and then conclude from this that stability prevails. This general stability is not in question; however, the empirical significance of the percentage changing is largely neglected. If that rate of change occurs year after year, the cumulative effect is considerable. The issue here is a matter of emphasis. Claiming that most are stable is correct, but that claim detracts from understanding the effects of gradual but persistent change among a small segment of the electorate. Finally, focusing on just the issue of stability or nonstability distracts us from assessing whether those with views that are in conflict with an existing party identification might be gradually changing.

Assessing Voter Transitions

The idea that some voters are changing their party identifications and there is a transition process is simple to understand, but the process of detecting this transition is not so simple. Ideally we need to have information on an unchanging set of voters over a lengthy period of time. We also need for some our set of individuals to identify as Democrats or Republicans and for each party to have some diversity of views about public policy issues. We could then track those who initially identified as Democrats, but have conservative views, and compare their party identification over time with Democrats holding liberal views. We could also track those who initially identified as Republicans, but have liberal views, and compare them with Republicans who held conservative views. Presumably the conservative Democrats would gradually move to identify with the Republican Party, and liberal Republicans would gradually move to identify with the Democratic Party. The crucial matter is that the transition process would result in a relatively temporary increase in the percentage of independents during the transition.

The difficulty is that we have no such information on a set of individuals over any appreciable length of time. The most widely used survey of US political opinions is that of the National Election Study (NES), which has been cited throughout this book. These studies, done every two years since 1948, consist primarily of a sample of voters within a particular year. In some years, the same set of voters was asked questions several times during the same year. Three times over the 1948–2002 time span, NES has tracked the same voters over multiple years. One study tracked the same voters from 1956 to 1960, another tracked the same voters from 1972 to 1976, and a third study followed the same voters from 1992 to 1996. These studies, discussed later in this chapter, are limited to only four years, however. Because party attachments do not change easily, studies covering only four years, as long-term party changes are occurring, provide only a suggestion of how change is proceeding. We simply do not have the ideal information that we would like to have to track how voters respond to change that takes years to unfold.

We are left with samples that provide portraits of voter opinions and party identification only within specific years. Those portraits or snapshots of the electorate, although enormously valuable in helping us understand American politics, have significant limitations as we try to understand change. First, they are not samples of the same people from year to year. Further, they are not even samples drawn from a constant pool of the electorate. Some voters die, and younger ones reach the age when they are eligible to vote. Immigrants enter our society and, after some delay, become naturalized and enter the pool of those eligible to register to vote. Thus, we are not tracking a particular set of voters nor are we drawing from a relatively constant pool of possible voters.

Again, we do not have the data necessary to properly track change in electoral reactions.

The consequence is that we must fall back to forming a theoretical expectation that suggests what patterns we should find in successive samples if change is proceeding as we anticipate. This is by no means a definitive test, but it is the best that can be done given the available data.

To conduct such an analysis, we need to distinguish voters experiencing conflict with their party from those who are not. In this case, we begin with opinions about the role that government should play in society. Again, the only question we have that is relevant to that issue over a lengthy period of time asks whether government should get involved in helping people get jobs. Over the last several decades, a major division has emerged over whether government should play a role or individuals should be responsible for their own situations within a society dominated by private markets. As reviewed in the prior chapter, this difference did not divide the parties until the mid-1960s. In subsequent years, the Republican Party has become increasingly dominated by those who oppose a role for government in this regard, whereas the Democratic Party has been divided.

If this issue were becoming more significant, we should see very different changes, depending on an individual's combination of opinion and party identification. Again, we are tracking categories of people (not the same people over time), and there should be changes within categories if issues are moving people. Over time, those individuals with views in conflict with the dominant views in their party should identify less with their party. Specifically, there should be a gradual decline in the percentage that oppose government involvement and identify with the Democratic Party, and there should also be a decline in the percentage that support government involvement and identify with the Republican Party. That is, changes in party identification should be selective.

If realignment were occurring, there should also be movement toward parties among those who find their views more compatible with the other party. Those who support a government role should be moving toward the Democratic Party, and those opposed to this role should be moving toward the Republican Party. For example, if someone opposed a government role, but initially identified with the Democratic Party, the movement should be a gradual shift into the category of leaning Democratic, then independent, then leaning Republican.

Table 7.3 presents the results of NES surveys since the 1950s. The top part of the table is a repeat of Table 7.1 and indicates the overall distribution of party identification responses within each decade. The important changes over time have been the widely noted decline in the percentages of those identifying as either Democrats or Republicans and the increase in the percentage of independents. Both parties have

Table 7.3 Party Identification Changes Overall and by Opinion on Role of Government, 1950s–2000s

	Democrat	Lean Dem.	Independent	Lean Rep.	Republican
All Respondents					
1950s	48.1	7.8	7.2	6.7	29.8
1960s	48.9	8.2	9.5	6.8	26.3
1970s	40.5	12.0	13.5	9.3	23.3
1980s	39.3	14.0	11.4	12.8	27.0
1990s	36.2	13.5	10.1	11.4	28.6
2000s	34.5	14.4	9.2	13.0	28.6
Change	−13.6	6.6	2.0	6.3	−1.2
Party identification for those believing government should help ensure jobs available					
1950s	54.0	6.5	8.3	5.1	25.6
1960s	59.5	9.6	7.6	3.9	19.2
1970s	53.3	15.1	12.3	6.3	12.4
1980s	53.5	13.5	13.2	7.4	18.3
1990s	50.3	16.1	10.3	8.4	14.6
2000s	51.3	18.0	8.7	7.8	14.1
Change	−2.7	11.5	0.4	2.7	−11.5
Party identification for those believing government should not help ensure jobs available					
1950s	36.7	6.9	7.4	10.0	38.2
1960s	39.2	9.2	11.1	9.3	33.3
1970s	31.3	11.5	13.9	13.2	29.9
1980s	28.6	12.7	13.2	17.5	35.8
1990s	25.6	11.2	8.5	14.8	39.8
2000s	24.4	12.8	7.9	16.9	37.9
Change	−12.2	5.9	0.5	6.9	−0.3

Source: NES Cumulative Data File, 1948–2002; years averaged, not pooled within decades.

Note: Results are aggregated within each decade. Decades are defined as: 1950s, 1952–1958; 1960s, 1960–1968; 1970s, 1970–1978; 1980s, 1980–1988; 1990s, 1990–1998; and 2000s, 2000–2002.

experienced declines, although the decline is much greater for the Democratic Party (Hetherington, 2001). As noted before, these data are the basis of the conventional conclusion that the attachment to parties is declining.

The rest of the chapter analyzes changes by issue positions, for those who think government should and should not be involved in this issue. Among those who believe government should be involved, identification with the Democratic Party (either strong or weak) declines only 2.7 percentage points, whereas identification with the Republican Party (strong or weak) declines 11.5 percentage points. The change was selective. Among those opposed to a government role, the change was also selective. There were 0.3 percent fewer identifying with the Republican Party and 12.2 fewer identifying as Democrats. Changes for each party were strongly related to opinions.

The central issue, however, is: If realignment is occurring, why does the percentage of independents increase? Changing party identification is not easy. There is clearly an affective component to party identification, with people's fundamental social identity tied up with their party identification. That means that declines in party identification are unlikely to quickly result in increases in party identification with the other party. Again, we do not have the data to track the same people over time, but we can form an expectation of the results if specific voters are moving in certain directions. If voters change slowly, then we would expect most of those rejecting a particular view to move gradually through the leaning/independence/leaning (toward other party) categories.

That expectation prevails for those supportive of, and opposed to, a role for government. For those supportive of a government role, from the 1950s to the 1970s there is a decline of 13.2 percentage points in identification as a Republican. Most of that change moves to the pure independent or leaning Democratic category, but not to identifying as a Democrat. Beginning in the 1980s, when the party differences were becoming clearer, the pure independent category begins to decline, and most of the change moves to the leaning Democratic category. A similar pattern prevails among those who oppose a government role, with the change playing out over several decades. There is a drop in Democratic identity beginning in the 1960s. That change moves first to the categories of leaning Democratic and independent. There is then an increase in the leaning Republican category. Democratic identification continues to drop during the 1980s and 1990s, and the percentage leaning Democratic remains at 11–12 percent, even as the percentage leaning Republican increases.

Overall, there is a significant movement away from the Democratic Party, with the change going into the independent or leaning categories, and not to full identification with the Republican Party.

This analysis can be refined by examining how cohorts of voters are behaving. Central to the debate about party identification is whether cohorts (those born in a specific era) form a party identification and do not change after a party identification is adopted. As noted earlier, we do not have data that allows us to track specific individuals over time. As an alternative, we can track the distribution within cohorts of party identification by opinions about government. Just as with the analysis of all voters considered together, the question is whether within each cohort there are changes in identification dependent on opinions about the role of government. For this analysis, the cohorts are again grouped as those born prior to 1930, from 1930 through 1949, and after 1950.[36]

For those born prior to 1930 (Table 7.4), a cohort that was heavily Democratic, there is a steady increase in Democratic and leaning Democrat identifications among those who support a government role. Those opposed to a role for government become less Democratic. Also for those opposed to a role for government, there is no increase (indeed, there is a small decrease) in identification (strong or weak) as Republican, but there is an increase in the percentage that lean Republican. Overall there is movement away from and to parties, with the movement largely reflecting a resorting based on different views of the role of government. Most important, among those who believe in a greater role for government, not all the movement away from Republican identification results in strong or weak identification with the Democratic Party. Some movement is only to leaning Democratic, resulting in a modest increase in independent identification among this cohort.

For those born between 1930 and 1949 (Table 7.4), the changes over time are greater. Among those who support a government role, Democratic identification increases significantly. There is a decline in the percentage identifying with or leaning Republican, and all of this decline emerges as identification with the Democratic Party. Among those opposed, there is a significant decline in the percentage identifying with or leaning to the Democratic Party. Not all of this decline, however, results in an increase in strong or weak Republican identification. There is a considerable increase in the percentage leaning Republican, which results in an overall increase in the percentage with-

Table 7.4   Party Identification Changes by Opinion on Role of Government, Those Born Prior to 1930 and Those Born 1930–1949

	Democrat	Lean Dem.	Independent	Lean Rep.	Republican
Born Prior to 1930					
Party identification for those believing government should help ensure jobs available					
1950s	54.7	6.1	7.7	5.2	26.2
1960s	60.2	6.7	7.9	3.9	21.3
1970s	60.1	9.8	8.9	4.8	16.3
1980s	62.0	8.5	6.5	6.0	17.0
1990s +	63.4	9.7	5.9	5.5	15.4
Change	8.7	3.6	−1.8	0.3	−10.8
Party identification for those believing government should not help ensure jobs available					
1950s	35.5	6.7	7.9	10.1	39.8
1960s	39.6	7.1	10.3	9.0	34.0
1970s	36.4	8.0	9.1	11.0	35.5
1980s	33.2	7.2	8.4	11.7	39.5
1990s +	32.2	8.6	8.6	13.6	37.1
Change	−3.3	1.9	0.7	3.5	−2.7
Born 1930–1949					
Party identification for those believing government should help ensure jobs available					
1950s	44.3	14.9	10.3	9.2	21.3
1960s	54.7	13.1	11.3	5.7	15.3
1970s	51.2	17.7	12.3	8.4	10.5
1980s	57.1	13.7	8.7	6.4	14.1
1990s +	57.3	14.8	7.7	7.0	13.3
Change	13.0	−0.1	−2.6	−2.2	−8.0
Party identification for those believing government should not help ensure jobs available					
1950s	45.2	14.3	9.5	9.5	21.4
1960s	39.4	13.5	11.0	11.2	24.9
1970s	26.0	13.7	16.6	16.1	27.6
1980s	28.9	10.9	10.0	16.4	33.7
1990s +	25.4	11.6	6.6	18.1	38.3
Change	−19.8	−2.7	−2.9	8.6	16.9

Source: NES Cumulative Data File, 1948–2002; years averaged, not pooled within decades.

Note: Results are aggregated within each decade. Decades are defined as: 1950s, 1952–1958; 1960s, 1960–1968; 1970s, 1970–1978; 1980s, 1980–1988; 1990s+, 1990–2002.

in this cohort that respond as independent when asked their party identification.

Finally, the cohort born since 1950 (Table 7.5) was coming to political awareness at a time when the differences between the parties were diminished and each party contained considerable diversity. This is also the cohort that saw the parties change. As might be expected, these voters were initially considerably less partisan than prior cohorts. The percentage defining themselves as independent during the 1970s was 51.3 overall. That cohort's contribution to an increase in the overall percent-

Table 7.5   Party Identification Changes by Opinion on Role of Government, Those Born 1950 and After

	Democrat	Lean Dem.	Independent	Lean Rep.	Republican
Born 1950 and After					
Party identification for those believing government should help ensure jobs available					
1970s	40.6	21.9	20.8	8.1	8.6
1980s	42.8	18.1	14.6	10.2	14.4
1990s +	44.5	18.7	12.2	9.7	14.9
Change	3.9	−3.2	−8.6	1.6	6.3
Party identification for those believing government should not help ensure jobs available					
1970s	29.3	17.9	22.1	13.1	17.7
1980s	23.1	11.0	12.6	16.9	36.5
1990s +	22.7	12.6	9.3	14.8	40.6
Change	−6.6	−5.3	−12.8	1.7	22.9

Source: NES Cumulative Data File, 1948–2002; years averaged, not pooled within decades.

Note: Results are aggregated within each decade. Decades are defined as: 1950s, 1952–1958; 1960s, 1960–1968; 1970s, 1970–1978; 1980s, 1980–1988; 1990s+, 1990–2002.

age of independents did not come from a decline in partisan identification over time, but through their entrance into the electorate with low partisan identification.

This cohort was not only more independent, but it was also not divided by issues when they entered the electorate. Those who supported a role for government were 40.6 percent Democratic and 8.6 percent Republican, whereas those opposed were 29.3 percent Democratic and 17.7 percent Republican. Democratic identification was higher for those supporting a role for government, but Democrats also had an advantage in enrollment among those opposed to a role for government. By the 1990s, those opposed to a role for government had moved away from Democratic identification and toward Republican identification, resulting in a growing division in party identification by issue. As this cohort aligned with parties based on their issue position, the percentage of independents (both "pure" and those leaning to a party) steadily declined, contributing to an overall decline in the presence of independents in the electorate.

Summary

The percentage of the electorate defining themselves as partisan declined during the 1960s and the 1970s. This decline in partisan identification was generally interpreted as reflecting a growing disengagement by voters from parties. The recent decline in independents cannot be explained by the decline-of-parties argument, however, because that view provides no explanation as to why partisan identification should gradually increase. The more plausible explanation of changes over the last fifty years is that the changes reflect a gradual realignment. Voters reacted to the evolving concerns and images of the parties and gradually sorted themselves out according to their views of the role government should play. But during the transition of party bases, while voters were responding to change, many voters appeared to be independents as they changed their identifications from one party to another. To restate an earlier point, this increase in independents does not reflect a rejection of parties, but a gradual resorting of the electorate because voters are concerned about the match between their views and their partisanship.

8

The Future of Partisanship

Over the last fifty years, three major indicators of partisan attachment have followed the same pattern of at first decreasing and then increasing beginning in the 1980s. The percentage of House districts with split outcomes for presidential and House results initially rose, but has fallen since the late 1980s. Ticket-splitting rose during the 1960s and 1970s and has declined since then. The presence of self-identified independents rose during the same time period and is now gradually declining.

These trends are important, and we need to explain them. They are important for what they tell us about how change occurs and how partisanship is likely to evolve in the future.

With regard to explaining the changes, only a summary need be presented here. All these trends can be explained as reflections of realignment. House district results were following presidential results, but with a considerable lag and with incumbency playing a major role in slowing down the process of convergence of results. As convergence occurred, split outcomes declined. Split-ticket voting rose because many voters were experiencing a conflict between their policy views and their party identification. As that conflict subsided, either because of the realignment of voters, or because the intensity of an issue subsided, ticket-splitting declined. The presence of independents in the electorate rose as existing cohorts responded and as newer cohorts struggled to make sense of parties in flux. Those who had prior choices about party identification were shifting in accordance with their views of the role of government. As the images of the parties became clearer, the new cohorts sorted themselves out between the parties based on their views of the role of government, reducing the presence of independents. The changes in partisan attachments were following the pattern we would expect if gradual realignment were occurring.

This process of party change and electoral response has been lengthy, and it tells us much about how political change occurs. Much of our interpretation of American politics has stemmed from a focus on critical realignments (Burnham, 1970) and the analysis of the resulting party systems (Sundquist, 1983). This approach focuses on accumulations of conflict and relatively abrupt changes in party loyalties by voters. The alternative approach is to focus on gradual changes and secular realignment (Black and Black, 1987; 2002) and to presume that voters gradually sort out changes in the political context and gradually change their party identifications and voting in response.

The evidence from this analysis suggests that, at least for the last fifty years, change is of the latter nature. Voters do not follow politics closely, party positions change gradually, and voters only gradually respond to change. Party identifications are strong attachments, and we should expect only some voters to change parties and for changes to be incremental. The image of critical realignments as high-drama moments of intense issue assessment and abrupt alignment with parties has little relevance in explaining the aggregate changes of the last fifty years reviewed here. If there is a larger lesson about parties and change in this analysis, it is that historical analyses of change should receive more attention.

The Future

Even though the process of realignment is gradually increasing the extent of partisan attachment and partisan behavior within the electorate, the levels of partisan attachment now are not equivalent to the levels that prevailed at mid-century and earlier. The percent of House districts with split outcomes is still higher than in the early 1900s. Ticket-splitting is still somewhat higher now than it was in the 1950s. The percentage of independents (whether measured as initial responses or pure independents) is now higher than it was in the 1950s.

The question is what these trends are likely to be in the future. If the parties continue to attract constituencies central to their current concerns and to lose those that are uncomfortable with their central concerns, then over time the parties will become more homogenous internally. This process of building on their core constituencies is likely to prompt activities that further increase partisanship in the electorate.

At the district level, with a more polarized electorate, the parties will increasingly focus on mobilizing their constituents to try to win congressional seats. As incumbents retire, each party will become more capable of capitalizing on the partisan sentiment within the district, and each should be more effective at producing a match between presidential and House results. As that process unfolds, the extent of split outcomes should decline in subsequent years.

At the individual level, as voters gradually realign, those who hold views about basic issues of the role of government, about the appropriateness of social programs, about tax levels and the distribution of tax burdens, and about issues of the environment, equal opportunity, and cultural issues should gradually sort themselves out between the two parties, resulting in a decline in independents. Over time, there should be fewer cases of voters who identify with a party but also hold policy views that are contrary to the dominant views in that party. With the spread of competition into the South, more voters should be presented with House candidates compatible with their views. Together these changes should reduce split-ticket voting. As more voters engage in straight-ticket voting, partisan attachments should increase over time.

Nothing, of course, is certain in politics. As Bensel (2000) and James (2000) document, before and after 1900 the Democrats were seeking new constituencies to create a new majority. Party leaders regularly seek new constituencies, and those efforts could diminish our current polarization and reduce partisanship. There are also events, or demographic and social trends, or the changing composition of the electorate that may disrupt whatever partisan balance exists (Sundquist, 1983) and create new patterns of realignment that reduce partisanship. For example, US society is experiencing a significant increase in immigration and in the percentage of those who define themselves as nonwhite. These new entrants could tilt the balance toward Democrats or express their faith in individualism and upward mobility and support Republicans (Stonecash, 2002). Whether either trend reinforces or diminishes partisanship remains to be seen. Parties continually adapt to change, and they may adjust their appeals as change occurs, which could affect partisanship.

Although the changes noted above are possible, the current demographic trends and issues seem fairly stable and likely over the next decade or so to divide voters as they are now. Inequality is increasing, and those who are more affluent are not inclined to support a broad array of government efforts to change that. Cultural issues involve fundamental matters of morality and personal responsibility, and divisions about these issues seem unlikely to decline. To the extent that these issues remain dominant and that the parties use them as means to mobilize voters, the current realignment process is likely to continue, and partisan attachments are likely to grow stronger.

Appendix A:
The Role of Closeness of Elections

One possible explanation of an increase in split outcomes is a simple one. A split outcome is a case in which two different parties win the House and the presidential outcomes within a district. As Cummings notes and documents, split outcomes are more frequent when a presidential candidate's vote is relatively close to 50 percent (Cummings, 1966: 50–53). When the presidential vote is around 50 percent, it does not take a House vote that is very different in vote percentage to create a split outcome. There could be an increase in split outcomes if more House districts have voting results that cluster around 50 percent for both offices. If that occurs, then modest differences between vote results for the House and presidential candidates could occur, but one might be slightly above 50 percent and the other slightly below 50 percent. That would produce a split outcome, but there would be a small difference in the voting percentages.

Given the extent of regionalism in the first half of the twentieth century, many districts were heavily Democratic or Republican. Voting percentages for the two offices may not have been close, but because the district was so heavily inclined toward one party, the district still went to the same party. That is, the Democratic presidential candidate might receive 60 percent and the Democratic House candidate 90 percent The percentages are not similar, but there is no split outcome. With regionalism becoming less pronounced over time, elections may generally become more competitive, with more voting results clustering around 50 percent. Voting percentages could be more similar, but with results clustered around 50 percent, small differences could produce split outcomes.

Table A.1 indicates ways in which the joint distribution of House

Table A.1   Possible Distributions of Joint Presidential–House Outcomes

Presidential Vote %	Situation A: Democratic House %			Situation B: Democratic House %			Situation C: Democratic House %		
	< 40	40–60	>60	< 40	40–60	>60	< 40	40–60	>60
< 40	33			20			10	5	15
40–60		33			60		5	25	10
> 60			33			20	10	5	15

and presidential results might be distributed over time. The table presents three possible distributions of joint vote results. The groupings to the left and along the top indicate the vote percentage received by Democratic presidential and House candidates, respectively. Along the left is the distribution for presidential candidates. Along the top are the same groupings, but for House candidates in this case. Three distributions are presented. The numbers in the cells are the distribution percentages of districts that meet the two conditions. In situation A, for example, 33 percent of all House districts have outcomes in which the Democratic presidential and House candidates received less than 40 percent of the vote.

Situation A represents the early 1900s, when percentages for one office were matched by a similar percentage for the other office. Almost all cases were distributed along the diagonal running from the upper left to the lower right of that portion of Table A.1. If viewed as a scatterplot (see Figure 1.1), results for one office closely tracked the results for the other office. Much of the lower-right-hand corner was for results from the South, where Democrats won with high percentages. As regionalism declines, the distribution of cases could move to situation B or situation C.

Situation B represents what would happen if a higher percentage of joint outcomes were in the 40–60 percent range. If this happened, the possibility of more districts clustering around 50 percent could occur, creating the possibility of more split outcomes. This situation represents the possibility that more districts are experiencing closer outcomes.

If situation C occurs, a much lower percentage of cases are distributed along the diagonal, confirming that there is less association between results. For example, in this situation, in 15 percent of all districts the Democratic presidential candidate received less than 40 percent, and the Democratic House candidate received more than 60 percent. If situation C has occurred, it does not answer the question of why this occurred, but it does indicate that the possibility of situation B can be ruled out.

Considering these possibilities, Table A.2 reports information on the percentage of split outcomes, the percentage of presidential and House outcomes in the 40 percent to 60 percent category, and then the percentage with that joint outcome. This is then followed by the percentage of all outcomes in which both party candidates received greater than 60 percent (the upper left and lower right cells in Table A.1). The

Table A.2   Distribution of Closeness of Presidential and House Results

		District vote between 40 and 60% for:				
	% Split	Pres elections	House elections	Both	Both 60% +	On Diagonal
1900	3.3	55.7	51.8	45.6	38.0	83.6
1904	1.9	27.0	29.2	21.0	64.9	85.9
1908	6.0	46.9	47.8	38.6	43.9	82.5
1912	24.4	42.8	40.6	31.7	48.0	79.7
1916	10.9	63.1	48.3	47.3	35.4	82.7
1920	2.4	28.1	29.0	22.8	64.8	87.6
1924	8.3	19.7	27.6	13.8	64.6	78.4
1928	19.1	38.4	31.7	19.1	47.4	66.5
1932	13.2	50.0	49.7	43.2	42.5	85.7
1936	14.6	44.2	43.3	37.1	45.7	82.8
1940	12.5	55.7	42.5	40.6	40.6	81.2
1944	7.9	54.4	38.5	36.7	43.2	79.9
1948	17.7	62.9	42.9	40.0	24.8	64.8
1952	19.4	48.5	37.1	28.8	40.6	69.4
1956	29.4	48.3	41.8	25.3	32.7	58.0
1960	25.2	66.8	44.6	38.4	24.1	62.5
1964	33.8	40.0	43.7	24.6	36.1	60.7
1968	25.5	43.7	32.9	19.1	29.2	48.3
1972	43.7	26.0	26.7	6.4	31.9	38.3
1976	29.4	75.2	31.3	25.8	19.1	44.9
1980	33.6	49.0	30.3	13.6	27.2	40.8
1984	45.9	41.9	25.8	10.6	33.8	44.4
1988	34.1	59.5	15.4	9.7	30.8	40.5
1992	23.9	49.9	40.7	24.1	30.2	54.3
1996	23.2	66.4	36.8	33.3	29.9	63.2
2000	20.5	56.6	21.8	18.6	38.9	57.5

Source: Data compiled by the author.

last column of Table A.2 reports the percentage of all outcomes along the diagonal in Table A.1 (discussed above).

If an increase in split outcomes is a result of more joint outcomes clustering around 50 percent, then the percentage of districts with both outcomes greater than 40 percent and less than 60 percent of the vote should rise from the late 1950s through the 1980s, when the percentage of split outcomes was at its highest. In fact, the percentage of jointly close outcomes follows the opposite pattern from what we might expect. It generally is lower during the time period from the late 1950s through the 1980s. Further, the dominant pattern during the time of higher split outcomes was that results were simply dispersing more—the scatterplot was becoming less of a diagonal and more of a round scatter (see Figure 1.2). This is evident from the last two columns and Table A.2. The data for the one labeled "both 60 % +" gradually and erratically decline after 1944, and the final column also shows a steady decline after 1944, with a rise beginning in 1992.

The conclusion is that the increase in split outcomes is not a product of more elections clustering around the 50 percent point. There has been greater dispersion of House results around presidential results. This takes us back to the initial question: Why did this dispersion rise and then fall during the last decade?

Appendix B:
Data by House Districts

The creation of a reasonably correct data set for both House and presidential election results was fairly involved. Even with absolute care that the results are correct, an error occasionally appears. Further, there can be disputes about what a "correct" score is for some elections. The discussion here addresses the creation of the House data set first and then the presidential data set is discussed.

House Election Results

The accuracy of House election results is generally not discussed, but it is very relevant for this study. To the extent analyses are based on Inter-university Consortium for Political and Social Research (ICPSR) study 7757, accuracy issues are very important. We began with a comparison of the data from this ICPSR study with the election results printed in the *Congressional Quarterly's Guide to U.S. Elections, Volume II,* (2001) (hereafter *CQ Guide*), which revealed numerous errors. We first consulted the *CQ Guide* to determine the results for a particular district. Although the *CQ Guide* is very valuable, some third-party candidacies are not reported in that compilation. In some cases, the vote percentages reported are not based on all the votes actually cast in a district for House candidates. To remedy that problem, we consulted *United States Congressional Elections, 1788–1997* (Dubin, 1998). This is a remarkable publication, which has a depth of detail that is impressive. An incredible amount of work went into compiling this book.

Assuming Michael Dubin (1998) is accurate, several types of errors in the ICPSR data set were detected and corrected. In some cases, the percentage for the Democrat or Republican candidate was missing. In other cases, a percentage was recorded for a Democrat or Republican, but that candidate actually received no votes.

One kind of "error" in the ICPSR file is particularly noteworthy. In both California and New York, cross-endorsement of candidates has occurred; it continues to occur in New York. In California, a candidate might run with the endorsement of both the Democratic and Republican parties. In these cases, Dubin (1998) records the votes cast on each party endorsement line of a candidate. We were able to verify the actual party affiliation (not endorsements) of candidates by checking their affiliation in the prior Congress, by either using results for prior elections or consulting the Congressional Biographical Guide at http://bioguide.congress.gov/biosearch/biosearch.asp. In the ICPSR data set, many of these districts have no recorded votes, and thus these districts are missing from analyses of vote percentages. In New York, candidates can be cross-endorsed and then their names are listed on both party lines. We checked these cases against the official results printed in the *Legislative Manual* for various years. Although the votes on the separate lines should be added together and recorded as only a Democratic or Republican vote, the ICPSR data set records the vote on the Democratic line as the vote for the Democratic candidate and the vote on the Republican line as the vote for the Republican candidate. The result is that a district is recorded as contested and competitive to some degree, when it actually was uncontested by a major party candidate. Races were thus recorded as closer than they were. In both of these states, we corrected the data. In California, we used Dubin (1998) or the *Congressional Biographical Guide* designation of the candidate's actual party affiliation, recorded the total votes for the candidate on all party lines on the candidate's "true" party line, and recorded the other party line as 0. The logic of this approach is that the general concern is the partisan vote for major party candidates. In each district, almost all candidates will have an initial party affiliation, which will be known in the district. If the candidate receives the endorsement of another party, the actual vote is still for a candidate of a specific party. The same logic applies for New York. While a name is listed on two (or more) lines, the party affiliation of each candidate is well known, and the vote is for that candidate, regardless of the line on which it is received.

A similar issue involves Minnesota voting. For years, the Democrat-Farmer-Labor (DFL) Party served as the vehicle representing the Democratic Party in that state. The ICPSR shows no vote for

Democratic candidates in the years that the DFL was relevant. We recorded the DFL percentages as the Democratic vote. Again, the concern is not the vote percentage recorded on a party line, but the vote percentage that a candidate of a major party received.

Results in Louisiana present a particularly difficult issue concerning how to record results. For some years, Louisiana held an open primary in which all party candidates could enter. If no candidate received a majority, a runoff would be held between the two candidates with the highest percentages, even if they were from the same party. If a candidate did receive a majority in the primary, that individual's name would appear on the ballot on the traditional Tuesday in November without any apparent opposition. There would then be no recorded votes, making it difficult to record a result. If a candidate received enough votes to avoid a runoff, the apparent result in November is 0 (no votes) or 100 percent, for no opponent. Neither option, however, necessarily reflects the vote proportion that the candidate won in the open primary. In a study of vote percentages of members of Congress, the options of 0 or 100 percent are not satisfactory indicators of the situation the candidate faced.

These races might simply be excluded in a study, but that also is not very satisfactory. An option is to return to the results from Dubin (1998), which present both the open primary and runoff results. In many of these districts, several Democrats ran along with several Republicans, and the winning percentage for a Democratic candidate might be only 30 percent, compared to 13 percent for a Republican. Because this particular study concerns the vote proportion of candidates and their relative security, the decision in this case was to record the percentages of the leading Democrat and that of the leading Republican. This is not completely satisfactory because, for example, the leading Democrat might receive 30 percent, followed by another Democrat with 22 percent, and then a Republican with 13 percent. Recording only the leading Democrat and Republican will underrepresent the closeness of the second-highest vote recipient. (This is also a potential issue in a state such as California, where the second-highest vote recipient could run on the Progressive Party, and not show up if only Democrats or Republicans are recorded.) While this is a problem, it is minor because the focus in these vote records is on the proportion of winners, and the practice of recording 30 and 13 will reflect the percentage of the winner. The virtue of recording these percentages is that the winner actually received only 30 percent, which is not a secure position. Accurately recording and reflecting that low percentage seems appropriate in this case, and that is what was done. If a candidate was unopposed in the open primary, the candidate is recorded as unopposed and receiving 100 percent of the vote.

The problems in California and Minnesota may not affect results for members of Congress if those doing data runs took care to record the vote for winners, regardless of the party lines involved. If, however, a district were recorded as having a Democratic or Republican winner, but no percentages are recorded on the Democratic or Republican line, then these districts may show up as missing in an analysis. It is not possible to tell whether this occurred because most studies contain no discussions of these specifics. In New York, the problem could create clear percentage errors. If a cross-endorsed Democrat in New York City has his vote across two lines, his vote proportion might be interpreted as 65, when the actual percentage is 95 and there is no major opponent. If only contested races are assessed, the New York situation will lead to this district being included, when it should have been excluded. Again, it is unknown whether this problem actually occurred in published studies because there is no discussion of such an issue.

Another important issue concerns how to record at-large contests when there are multiple seats involved. Although the winners can easily be recorded, there is the issue of what percentage to record for the winner and the opponent. The goal here is to record the competitiveness of elections, so with that in mind, the winner with the highest percentage is recorded and paired with the major party losing opponent with the highest percentage. The next-highest winner is then paired with the next-highest major party losing candidate. For example, in Illinois in 1916 the winning Republican, McCormick, was given 54.4 percent and was paired with the most successful losing Democrat, Williams, 42.0 percent.

Finally, there is a potential problem with a number of contested elections. If someone was listed as winning in the initial counts, but an investigation about charges of incorrectly counted results resulted in a corrected outcome and corrected score, reported at a later date, the corrected results were recorded rather than the initial results.

Presidential Election Results

The presidential election results were taken largely from two sources. Results from 1952 through 2000 were taken from various

Congressional Quarterly (CQ) reference books or reports or other sources such as various editions of the *Almanac of American Politics*. In some years, CQ reported the results in March of the year following the presidential election. In other cases, CQ published the results in *Congressional Districts in the 1980s* or *Congressional Districts in the 1990s*. For a few years, the results were available only in editions of *Almanac of American Politics*. The 2000 results were obtained directly from CQ. The results for 1900–1948 come from a project on which Peter Nardulli has been working. He is gratefully acknowledged for his generously sharing these data with us. Nardulli compiled data on presidential results by county, and by using information from *The Historical Atlas of United States Congressional Districts, 1789–1983* (Martis, 1982) on which counties comprise each House district, he aggregated county presidential results to the congressional district level and recorded presidential results by congressional district. A complete explanation of how these data were compiled is available at http://www.pol.uiuc. edu/nardulliresearch.html under "Appendix I: Local Electorates: Data Sources and Methodological Procedures."

This procedure of grouping counties by congressional district also makes it possible to aggregate population and land area for House districts, and then calculate the density per House district. It is not possible to do this, however, for counties that are part of a district or counties that contain more than one district. The latter are all highly populated urban counties (e.g., Suffolk County [Boston], Massachusetts; New York City; Baltimore, Maryland). The result is that presidential results and density scores are not available for these counties. See endnote 10 for a more complete discussion of this problem and attempts to cope with it.

Split-Outcome Results

Nardulli's presidential results and demographic data were merged with the House results by House district. This makes it possible to cover much of the same time frame covered by Cummings (1966: 31–39) in his analysis of House–presidential results over time.

The resulting calculation of the number of split-outcome districts is somewhat different from the standard results presented. The conventional year-by-year data on split outcomes are presented in *Vital Statistics on American Politics, 2001–2002* (Stanley and Niemi, 2001:

46). The data for this publication come from prior editions of *Vital Statistics,* which were taken from Burnham (1970: 109). Burnham indicates that his data for 1920–1964 came from Cummings (1966: 10), and to derive the results for 1900–1916, he "extended" Cummings' analysis. Two problems arise in trying to explain any discrepancies between the results we report and the results of Cummings and Burnham. Cummings provides no discussion of just how the data in his book were derived, but does indicate that the data were obtained from Ruth Silva, a faculty member at the Pennsylvania State University. It is unknown, however, whether she used a file from the ICPSR (which currently has numerous errors) or whether Silva created her own data set. In private communication in 2002, Cummings indicated that the data had long been lost, and he could not remember just how the results were calculated. Ruth Silva is deceased, and no one at the Department of Political Science at Penn State is familiar with her data set. The books published by Silva contain no reference to any analyses using these data. It appears that, although she spent what must have been an enormous amount of time assembling the data set, given the difficulties of acquiring these data in the late 1950s and early 1960s, she never used the data set herself. Burnham provides no explanation of how he "extended" Cummings's analysis, so it is not possible to compare the two sets of results.

The results from *Vital Statistics* on split outcomes and the derived results can therefore be compared in the aggregate only. That is, district-by-district comparisons cannot be performed to see where discrepancies occurred because there is no database or report for such a comparison. Table B.1 indicates the total number of House districts in the House of Representatives, the number and percentage of split outcomes according to *Vital Statistics,* and the author's calculations for the number of districts for which both presidential and House results could be obtained for the data set used for this analysis, the resulting percentage of districts with split outcomes (among those districts with both results), and the number of districts not included due to missing presidential results. The number of districts for which presidential results cannot be determined increases somewhat steadily from 1900 through 1948.

Almost all of these missing districts involve situations in which a county has such a large population that it becomes a multidistrict county. Most other congressional districts consist of one or more counties, so it is possible to add county results. For multidistrict counties, historical

Table B.1 Data on Split Outcomes from *Vital Statistics* and Derived by the Author

Year	Total # districts	From *Vital Statistics* Number	Percentage	Calculated by Author Number	Percentage	Missing
1900	357	295	3.4	302	3.3	55
1904	386	310	1.6	314	1.9	72
1908	391	314	6.7	316	6.0	75
1912	435	333	25.2	324	24.4	111
1916	435	333	10.5	321	10.9	111
1920	435	344	3.2	337	2.4	98
1924	435	356	11.8	338	8.3	97
1928	435	359	18.9	340	19.1	95
1932	435	355	14.1	289	13.2	146
1936	435	361	14.1	323	14.6	112
1940	435	362	14.6	319	12.5	116
1944	435	367	11.2	315	7.9	120
1948	435	422	21.3	310	17.7	125
1952	435	435	19.3	433	19.4	2
1956	435	435	29.9	435	29.4	0
1960	437	437	26.1	437	25.2	0
1964	435	435	33.3	435	33.8	0
1968	435	435	32.0	435	25.5	0
1972	435	435	44.1	435	43.7	0
1976	435	435	28.5	435	29.4	0
1980	435	435	32.8	435	33.6	0
1984	435	435	45.0	429	45.9	0
1988	435	435	34.0	434	34.1	0
1992	435	435	23.0	435	23.9	0
1996	435	435	25.5	435	23.2	0
2000	435	435	19.8	435	20.5	0

records that include House and presidential results by precinct or election district may allow presidential results to be assigned to a district. It is costly to acquire these data, however, but even though doing so is likely to be very difficult, it seems imperative that they be acquired at some time. These multidistrict county results are crucial because they represent the urban areas, which were of growing importance during the last century. These are also the areas in which Republicans did well during the late 1800s and early 1900s, and there was then a major reversal of fortunes with Democrats doing well (Eldersveld, 1949; Degler, 1964; Turner and Schneier, 1970: 118). These data will allow us to understand how that change played out.

Appendix C:
Measurement Error and Partisanship

The most significant criticism of the presumption that voters change their party identification over time comes from several works by Donald Green and his colleagues, who argue that party identification measures contain errors (Green and Schickler, 1993) and that most of the "apparent" change is really measurement error. They contend that once the measurement error is corrected, much of the systematic change disappears, and the association between political opinions and changes in party identification diminishes dramatically (Green, 1991; Green and Palmquist, 1990, 1994). This is a technical debate, but one with enormous significance for our understanding of how change occurs in US politics. Green builds his analysis on prior works by Heise (1969), Wiley and Wiley (1970), and Asher (1974). The crucial matters about these works involve the assumptions each of them makes about differences in responses over time.

Heise (1969) and Wiley and Wiley (1970) are primarily concerned about how to handle measurement error in panel data or surveys in which the same respondents are asked the same (and more) questions over time. That is, respondents are found and interviewed and then reinterviewed at a later date. The concern is whether respondents may be inclined to respond randomly, creating error in measuring respondents' views over time.

Heise (1969) proposes a method of analysis for measurement error. The interesting matter is how his analysis deals with systematic change, such as a voter moving slightly from one party identification position to another and then remaining "changed." His analysis seems to preclude incorporating change in responses that persists. It also appears to

145

exclude an examination of factors that might create that change. He introduces a variable u as "the aggregation of variables that have affected or disturbed x during the interval from 1 to 2" (p. 95), but then it disappears from the analysis. It is as if he acknowledges "disturbances," but then they disappear. Then he states under "restrictions" that "measurement errors at different times are uncorrelated with each other." This is perhaps the most important step in the analysis. It appears that "measurement error" is the difference in a score from time 1 to 2 to 3 in a panel data set. If that is the case, Heise is assuming that observations do not change steadily in one direction (away from or toward a party). If someone who holds liberal positions but is in the Republican Party consistently moves more Democratic during a panel study, that creates change, but this seems to be an error in his analysis. If treated as such, these people would produce errors correlated with each other over time. That is, someone's deviation from their "true" score at time $t - 1$ would be associated with their deviation at time t and time $t + 1$. Although what is an error is not clearly stated in Heise's analysis, it does seem that u disappears from the analysis after that. Apparently, his procedure is to assume away systematic change, and therefore there is no need to pursue what effect u might have, or what could be creating that systematic change. He then goes on to derive a formula that uses existing correlations and never introduces u factors as a source of change in x values.

Wiley and Wiley (1970) repeat the assumption that "measurement errors are serially uncorrelated" (p. 113), as does Asher (1974), when he states that "the measurement errors at different time points are uncorrelated" (p. 478). Asher then goes on to note that "the third assumption may be somewhat dubious" given the specific context.

It seems that the practice is, much as with discussions of ordinary least squares (OLS), to list the assumptions that make an estimator the best linear unbiased estimator (BLUE), and then proceed as if the assumptions are met, often without doing the analysis to verify the assumptions.

As an example of focusing only on the randomness explanation and approach to analysis, Dreyer (1973) notes that in the 1956–1960 NES panel study, individuals do change. He finds that from 1956 to 1958, 39 percent change; from 1958 to 1960, 40 percent change; and from 1956 to 1960, 43 percent change (pp. 718–720). He then divides respondents into those changing and those not. He treats all those who changed as likely random changers, and conducts a test to assess whether randomness is a plausible explanation of changes. He concludes, "By and large the only change that occurred over this period was random change" (p. 721). Two matters are notable. First, stability is emphasized ("by and large") rather than focusing on the extent of change. Second, no assessment is made of whether changes might correlate with specific attitudes. Only randomness is assessed.

Then there is the issue of the basis of the correction formulas. Their basis appears to be that we accept the fact that no systematic disturbance factors are operating, so we can focus only on the correlations among the true scores, and we do not have to conduct an analysis that incorporates any exogenous factors, such as issues. There is an alternative way change could be analyzed. If survey respondents have changes in party identification, those changes could be correlated with changes in opinion on issues to see if the two are correlated. This analysis is not done. Rather, assumptions are made, and then scores are "corrected," thereby eliminating change.

All of this becomes important when we move to Green's analysis. Green introduces aggregate data and focuses on general stability (avoiding noting that some change does occur), cites Heise (1969) and Wiley and Wiley (1970), introduces disturbance terms (Green and Palmquist, 1990: 878), but then apparently any focus on disturbance terms disappears. He then corrects for measurement error (treating any change as representing measurement error) and concludes that short-term forces as a source of change are of little significance. The result is a repeat of the practices of Heise and Wiley and Wiley. Sources of disturbance are acknowledged and noted, but largely dismissed as something to assess.

Notes

1. The data, explained in Appendix B, Data by House Districts, were compiled from various sources. The actual percentage of the vote received by candidates is used, rather than the percentage of the two-party vote.

2. The number of studies pursuing these questions is vast. A full review of all these studies is contained in such works such as Jacobson, 2001; Stonecash et al., 2003: 131-150, and Stonecash, 2004. Typical studies include Abramowitz, 1979, 1989, 1991; Alford and Hibbing, 1981; Ansolabehere et al., 2000; Born, 1979, Campbell, 1983; Collie, 1981; Cover, 1977; Cover and Mayhew, 1977; Cox and Katz, 1996; Erickson, 1971, 1972, 1976; Ferejohn, 1977; Fiorina, 1981b; Johannes and McAdams, 1981; Krasno and Green, 1988; Krehbiel and Wright, 1983; Levitt and Wolfram, 1997; Nelson, 1978-79; Parker, 1980; Payne, 1980; Serra, 1994; Serra and Clover, 1992; Yiannakis, 1981.

3. Further, there is evidence that the ability of incumbents to increase their percentage of votes with each successive term in office is no greater now than it was during the first part of the century. The ability of incumbents to increase their vote percentages with successive years in office can be measured by assessing the relationship between vote percentage and years in office. That is, the regression is vote percentage in year 2 on year 2, vote percentage in year 4 on year 4, vote percentage in year 6 on year 6, and so on. The slope then measures the ability to increase the percentage received over time. Using this measure for all those first elected in 1900-1948 compared to all those first elected in 1950–2000, the rate of increase (slope) is less (.48 per year) for 1950–2002 than it is for 1900–1950 (.57) (Stonecash and Widestrom, 2004).

4. Much of the attention of realignment analyses has focused on critical, or abrupt, realignments (Key, 1955; Burnham, 1970; Sundquist, 1983). The focus on abrupt shifts in overall levels of support and in the electoral coalitions of each party has been criticized by Mayhew (2003) as being unproductive because the evidence in support of this interpretation is questionable. The concern here is not with critical or abrupt realignment, but with gradual shifts in which social groups support which party (Key, 1959) or secular realignment.

Critical realignments are in some ways easier to detect, assuming they exist: An "event" happens, and we can track shifts in party allegiances over some relatively short period of time. Secular realignment, in contrast, involves interpreting political changes over a longer period of time and creating a narrative that explains the sources of the gradual shifts.

5. The South is defined here as Alabama, Florida, Georgia, Kentucky, Louisiana, Mississippi, North Carolina, South Carolina, Tennessee, Texas, and Virginia. Some use a different definition of "South," including Arkansas and excluding Kentucky. This is the grouping used by V.O. Key in *Southern Politics*. The NES includes Delaware, Washington, D.C., West Virginia, and Oklahoma in the South and excludes Kentucky. I have serious doubts about adding Delaware, the District of Columbia, West Virginia, and Oklahoma as Southern states, as do others (Hadley, 1981: 400). I also find it difficult to think of Kentucky as a Northern state or as part of the West, so by default it ends up in the South. The questionable state is Arkansas. Analyses were run with Arkansas included and with it excluded, and the alternate groupings do not appreciably change the trends found.

6. House districts cannot be used over time because the boundaries shift roughly every ten years.

7. That is, the state partisan percentages for Democratic House candidates (all within each state aggregated) for 1904, 1908, 1912, and onward, are correlated with the state partisan percentage for House candidates in the 1900 election. This correlation tracks the relative position of states over time and how stable they are. The overall Democratic vote may rise or fall over time, but the correlation tracks the stability of the relative positions of states, relative to their 1900 position. For the presidential contest, the state-by-state results are used, and results for subsequent years are correlated with 1900. Results for 1900–1996 are taken from Rusk (2001: 158–170). The results for 2000 are taken from the Federal Election Commission (FEC) results presented on their web site: http://www.fec.gov/pubrec/fe2000/2000presge.htm.

8. While Carmines and Stimson (1984; 1989) suggest that 1964 was the year in which civil rights issues became a highly salient issue in US politics and caused a significant realignment of voting, this might more appropriately be regarded as the second major realignment associated with race issues. Although the authors acknowledge the civil rights efforts of President Truman, they do not devote any attention to the effects of his policies on presidential voting in the 1948 race, in which there was a clear shift in the Democratic presidential vote in the South.

9. The two exceptions to this are Maine and Nebraska, where two electors are chosen by statewide popular vote and the remainder by the popular vote within each Congressional district. See http://www.fec.gov/pages/ecworks.htm.

10. This correlation is flawed because from 1900 to 1948 the most urban districts are missing from the analysis. As Appendix B indicates, there are no presidential results by congressional district for many urban counties from 1900 to 1948. For counties that contain more than one House district, there are currently no data compilations available that provide a data breakdown within

the county such that presidential results by district can be calculated. This becomes a more serious problem because more of the population is in these urban counties (Suffolk [Boston], New York, Baltimore, Philadelphia, Pittsburgh, Cayuhoga [Cleveland], Wayne [Detroit], and Los Angeles). Because of this, in 1900 there were 55 districts without a presidential score, and by 1948 the number was 125, or more than one-fourth of the districts. These are the most urban districts, with the greatest density. Their absence creates a situation in which the districts with the highest density are not included in the analysis. If Democrats did relatively better in those districts, then the correlation would be more positive during the 1900–1948 time period. Lower Democratic success in those areas would reduce the correlation. So, missing scores are clearly a problem, but complete scores became available in 1952, and the change from an incomplete to complete data set did not produce a significant change in the correlation. Furthermore, if the districts with missing scores are coded as having the highest density scores and the correlation is rerun, the correlation results are not different. The conclusion is that higher density did not translate into relatively high Democratic success for most of the century. It was only in the 1980s that a significant difference developed.

Given the limitations of this data analysis-omitting the urban areas, which are presumably the districts in which Democrats made significant gains in 1928 and the 1930s—an attempt was made to substitute approximate values for the missing scores. There are two missing values in this analysis for the urban counties: the density within a district and the presidential vote. For a rough approximation of density, the density level for the entire county was used. That overstates density in some districts and understates it in others. Density, however, is much greater in these urban counties than in other counties, so using this "average" density places these districts at the high end of density. Although this may introduce an error, the relative placement of these districts on a density scale is appropriate. The graph on page 152 illustrates this point.

For an approximation of presidential values, the overall county percentage for Democratic presidential candidates was used. This also understates and overstates some values.

If the correlation of presidential results with density is calculated with these substituted values, the results are largely the same. In general, the correlation is more negative for the years 1900 to 1948. Democratic presidential candidates did better in more rural areas for the first half of the century, with the exception of 1928, when Al Smith was able to do well in urban areas and create a positive association of presidential results with density.

Perhaps the most puzzling aspect of this pattern is the modestly negative correlation in 1932 and 1936. Franklin Roosevelt is often portrayed as a Democrat who benefited enormously from an urban base (Eldersveld, 1949; Degler, 1964). Although he did well compared to his predecessors in 1932, 1936, and 1940 in districts with the higher density levels, he still did relatively better in districts with lower levels of density. The graph on page 153 presents the percentage of the vote received by Democratic presidential candidates by the density level of the districts from 1900 to 2000. For 1900–1948, the districts are grouped by population per square mile, with groupings of low (0–59), mid-

Correlation of Density and Democratic Presidential Percentages, with and Without Substituted Values, 1900–2000

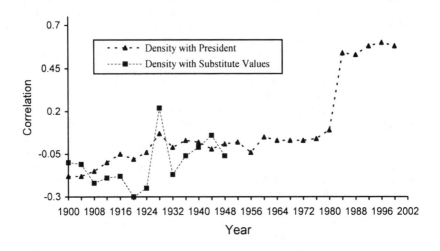

dle (60–999), and high (1,000+). For 1950–2000, these groupings are 0–99, 100–1,199, and 1,200+, respectively. Over time, the relative success by density levels reverses. In the 1932–1940 elections, Roosevelt's vote percentage increased in all categories, compared to the 1900–1924 period, but the relative level of success did not change, resulting in a negative correlation.

11. The 2000 census was the first one that allowed respondents to choose multiple races, so the results are not directly comparable to prior censuses. In the 2000 census, 47.9 percent of Hispanics (or Latinos) regarded themselves as white, 2.0 percent regarded themselves as black or African American, 42.2 percent regarded themselves as "some other race," and 6.3 percent regarded themselves as "two or more races." See the report "Overview of Race and Hispanic Origin, 2000," issued March 2001, available at http://www.census.gov/prod/2001pubs/c2kbr01-1.pdf.

12. Brady et al. (2004) counter the suggestion that the recent period of polarization is unique and state that "the recent period is instead a readjustment to preexisting patterns of polarization." This return is only in the sense that the differences in DW-nominate scores by party have diverged again. The bases of those differences have greatly changed from before.

13. This argument presents a contrast with that of Brady et al. (2004), who argue that race has displaced the class divisions of the 1950s. They argue that "the class-based New Deal era was fading as the American economy grew and the country became overwhelmingly middle class" (pp. 2–3). They suggest that the 1960s and 1970s were somewhat of a lull in polarization as a new issue (race) emerged to displace class. The argument of this analysis is that multiple divisions have grown and that class divisions in particular have grown (Stonecash, 2000).

Democratic Presidential Success by Level of Density, with Substituted Values, 1900–2000

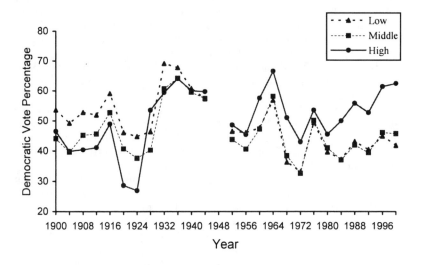

14. For this analysis, the DW-nominate scores are grouped as follows: –0.8 and less, greater than –0.8 to less than or equal to –0.6, greater than –0.6 to less than or equal to –0.4, and so forth.

15. Roberts and Smith (2003) provide an interesting analysis that suggests that the significant differences between the parties in the House did not develop until the 1980s. They argue that much of the increase in the 1970s was a reflection of the decision beginning in the early 1970s to include and record Committee of the Whole votes, which were more likely to involve amendments and represent conflicts.

16. There are two other ways to measure overlap. One is to add up all those members with an ADA score that overlaps with a score of the other party. Figure 4.5 does that and plots the total number with overlapping scores. The second approach calculates the percentage of "cross-pressured" members. Fleischer and Bond (2000b: 166) calculate the number of members within each party who are cross-pressured, or those with ideological preferences closer to the mean of the other party. They do this by using Americans for Democratic Action (ADA) and American Conservative Union (ACU) scores (pp. 184–185). They first calculate the average party score on these two measures, and then determine whether specific scores are closer to the mean of the member's party or the mean of the other party. The pattern for their results is similar.

17. The approach here is to accept the indicator of split outcomes as a legitimate and appropriate indicator deserving of explanation. Note, however, that the indicator overstates the extent to which results diverge. This indicator is an either-or indicator, and does not reflect the degree or extent of difference between results. A House district could be won by a House candidate with 51

percent of the vote, while the Democratic presidential candidate receives 49 percent of the vote, resulting in a two-point percentage difference and a split outcome. In contrast, in another district a Democratic presidential candidate could receive 49 percent while the Democratic House candidate received 85 percent, creating a difference of 36 percentage points. Both cases would be a split outcome, but the actual differences would be very different. The figure below indicates the average actual differences and the percentage of split outcomes from 1952 to 2000. The absolute average difference is used so that positive and negative differences are not canceled out, as would occur with the average difference.

This discrepancy between the percentage of split outcomes and the average absolute difference is true for the nation, the South, and the non-South. As the table on page 155 shows, for the non-South the difference between these two indicators has been significant for the last 50 years. The difference has also existed for the South for every year except for 1952.

18. The analysis presented here focuses on the same general topic as that addressed by Burden and Kimball (2002), that of split outcomes within particular election years rather than the rise and decline of such outcomes over time. They note the decline in split outcomes in the 1990s (p. 3) but then go on to focus primarily on variations in presidential–House partisan votes within any given year. Given that their focus of analysis is different (cross-sectional variations and the extent of individual-level split-ticket voting versus aggregate levels of split outcomes over time), the two analyses should not be expected to be similar. Nonetheless, their analysis and the one developed here present an interesting case of how two different frameworks can explain the same phenomenon

Percentage of House Districts with Split Presidential–House Outcome, 1952–2000

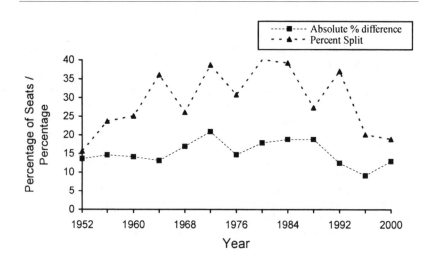

Percentage of Split Outcomes and Absolute Difference Between House and Presidential Percentages, by Year

	Nation		Non-South		South	
	Split	Difference	Split	Difference	Split	Difference
1952	19.1	13.6	14.6	6.9	31.6	32.6
1956	31.6	14.6	23.7	8.1	50.0	33.0
1960	28.6	14.1	25.1	6.9	38.6	34.4
1964	35.0	13.1	36.1	9.9	31.9	22.4
1968	37.0	16.9	26.1	9.5	68.1	38.1
1972	46.7	20.9	38.7	15.1	68.7	37.3
1976	28.5	14.7	30.8	12.8	22.3	20.1
1980	39.2	17.9	40.1	15.4	36.4	24.9
1984	44.2	18.8	39.3	14.8	56.6	28.1
1988	34.3	18.8	27.5	15.9	51.7	26.2
1992	39.2	12.5	37.0	11.7	44.2	14.5
1996	20.5	9.1	20.1	8.2	21.3	11.1
2000	19.4	13.0	18.9	11.3	20.8	17.0

very differently. There is no doubt that split outcomes rose and declined. The important matter, though, is what explains the increase. Burden and Kimball rely on the emergence of candidate-centered explanations and an increase in the incumbency effect to explain split outcomes (pp. 21–23 and pp. 161–163). They find that split outcomes are more likely when races are not competitive (p. 68). They also find that the most common cases of split outcomes are those in which a Republican presidential candidate runs ahead of a Democratic candidate (pp. 69–92). They then develop an analysis that finds that these differences (Republican president-Democratic House percentages) are likely to be greater when the Democratic candidate is an incumbent who has a significant advantage in campaign spending. They also note that Democratic candidates do better when they position themselves closer to the Republican presidential candidate (pp. 85–89). All of these explanations are plausible if a candidate-centered explanation is used to make sense of political trends.

The realignment perspective offers another way to see the same findings. First, there is the issue of why so many House districts have a Republican president and an incumbent Democratic House member (R - D situation). Although changes in the South are mentioned in Burden and Kimball's analysis (2002: 69–74), the primary emphasis is on explaining the differences in presidential–House candidate voting. The realignment perspective explains the emergence of these R - D situations as a consequence of the Republican presidential candidates steadily making inroads into conservative districts, with presidential candidates leading the way and House results following with a considerable time lag, on average. So, R - D situations are not so much a reflection of candidate-centered politics as the initiation of realignment.

Second, this development explains why House incumbent candidates survive when they have voting records close to that of presidential positions. If Republicans are more likely to do well in conservative districts, those districts are also likely to have House members who are more conservative. It is not the case that these members consciously positioned themselves to cope with Republican presidential candidates. The House members were already conservative.

Third, these R - D situations are more likely to occur in noncompetitive races because the established Democratic incumbents have considerable advantages in name recognition, and they are able to hold off the transition to Republican success at the House level for some time. This is, to be sure, a manifestation of candidate-centered politics, in that well-known and established incumbents can ward off partisan shifts. This ability persists as long as the incumbent is in office, but as the analysis presented here demonstrates, it is not a general phenomenon that persists after the incumbent who was present at the time of the transition leaves the scene. Incumbents slow down the transition, but they do not ward it off as a reflection of the general growth of the power of incumbency.

Finally, the campaign spending differential measure, although accurate, is a very flawed indicator and can be seen very differently from the realignment perspective. A great differential does not reflect great expenditures. Less-competitive House races result in less expenditure and particularly less for challengers against strong incumbents. A competitive race may involve both candidates raising more than $1 million with a close ratio of expenditures. A noncompetitive race may involve a ratio of $300,000 to $50,000, resulting in a high percentage of expenditure by the incumbent, but the advantage is in the ratio and not reflective of a high level of expenditure. Further, it is again only temporary before an incumbent retires and is replaced by a candidate from another party. In general, all the variables that Burden and Kimball (2002) find as being significant may also be seen as capturing situations in which a transition is occurring, an incumbent is warding off change, and the relationship dissipates over time as realignment unfolds.

Burden and Kimball (2002) do make an effort to create a dynamic interpretation of change at the end of their analysis. They argue that as the parties diverge and become more different, voters get more of a choice, and split-ticket voting declines (pp. 163–167), but the persistent argument in their analysis is that cross-sectional differences are due to the candidate-centered traits described above.

19. From a polling perspective, key to the incumbent are how many people have heard of them and what their reactions are. The standard question asked of voters is: "I'd like to read you the names of some people in public life. For each name, could you please tell me whether your impressions of that person are favorable or unfavorable? If you have never heard of someone, or don't have an opinion about someone, just say so." (Stonecash, 2003a: 82-88).

20. The trend data assembled by Erikson et al. (2002) for 1953 through the 1990s indicate how much the job approval of a president can vary over time within a presidential term and why member of Congress might be uneasy about being too closely identified with a president and having their votes tied to those for the president (p. 33). The change in George Bush's ratings over four years

provide further evidence of how much unpredictable fluctuations can occur. See http://www.washingtonpost.com/wp-srv/politics/daily/graphics/bush_approval_030704.html.

21. The level of the vote received by incumbents over time has received a great deal of attention but is not of concern here. (See Stonecash and Widestrom, 2004, for a critical review of this literature.)

22. There is also the possibility that the increase in the percentage of districts with split outcomes is largely a result of a "mathematical" change. If there are more House districts in which the House and presidential elections cluster around the 50 percent level, then relatively constant deviations of either presidential or House vote results could produce an increase in split outcomes because more cases cluster around the 50 percent point that determines a winner. The evidence does not support this interpretation. An analysis of the distribution of outcomes for each office and for joint outcomes for 1900–2000 is presented in the Appendix B.

23. An extensive literature exists, of course, on calculating the incumbency advantage over time. That literature focuses on the ability of incumbents to raise their visibility or vote percentage from some "normal" baseline. This might be assessed by comparing name recognition of incumbents versus non-incumbent winners or against challengers. It might be assessed by comparing the vote of a first-time winner with a sophomore, or the vote of a retiring incumbent with the vote percentage of the next first-time winner. Although an incumbency effect is another manifestation of the ability of a House member to affect his or her vote, the concern here is with split outcomes, so the concern is the House vote compared not to another House vote, but to the presidential vote.

24. These districts all involve cases for which a review of maps indicates that the location of the districts did not shift much. There may, of course, have been considerable change in the composition of the population and those registered to vote over time.

25. This stability of R^2 while the percentage of split outcomes fluctuated means that landslide elections for Democrats or Republicans shifted the overall level of partisan support for presidential candidates (i.e., raised or lowered the overall level, or intercept), whereas the relationships of demographic variables to vote percentages did not change much.

26. An independent is defined here as someone who responds to the initial question about identifying with a party in the NES surveys, and initially chooses independent. There are also independents who are often regarded as "pure" independents. These are the ones who, in the follow-up question, do not indicate they lean toward a party. Both types of independents will be examined in this and later chapters

27. This percentage ranges between 3 and 9 percent over this time period, with higher numbers prevailing until 1988.

28. This question has been asked three different ways over time. The specific wording and coding from the NES Codebook are presented below. The reference is to variable VCF0808 in the NES Cumulative Date File, 1948–2002:

Years 1956, 1958, 1960, 1964, 1968: "Should government guarantee jobs?"

Years 1956–1960: The introduction was the same as that used for VCF0805 (for years 1956, 1960, 1962), followed by: "The government in Washington ought to see to it that everybody who wants to work can find a job."

Years 1964, 1968: "In general, some people feel that the government in Washington should see to it that every person has a job and a good standard of living. Others think the government should just let each person get ahead on his own. Have you been interested enough in this to favor one side over the other?" [If yes:] "Do you think that the government . . ."

Variable VCF0809, 7-point govt guaranteed jobs scale:
Years 1972, 1974, 1976, 1978, 1980, 1982, 1984, 1986, 1988, 1990, 1992, 1994, 1996, 1998, 2000: "Some people feel that the government in Washington should see to it that every person has a job and a good standard of living."

Years 1972–1978, 1996 and later: "Suppose these people are at one end of a scale, at point 1."

"Others think the government should just let each person get ahead on their own. Suppose these people are at the other end, at point 7. And, of course, some other people have opinions somewhere in between, at points 2, 3, 4, 5 or 6."

"Where would you place yourself on this scale, or haven't you thought much about this?"

(A seven-point scale was presented to the respondent [see Table 6.1].)

29. This is not to say that elites shared this general agreement. As any history of 1940–1960 will show, Republican members of Congress during that era strongly supported business and opposed programs that would address problems of labor, education, and welfare. The concern here is party identifiers in the electorate.

30. There has been a general decline in straight-ticket voting within the Republican Party over time, suggesting that something other than this issue is affecting party support. This may be a response to the higher ideological cohesion of the Republican Party (Stonecash, 2000: 65, 79), which creates more unease among some Republicans.

31. Table 6.4 covers only 1976–2000 because those are the only years for which the NES Cumulative Data Files records the situation that each respondent faced. The data are pooled, rather than presented by decade to show changes over time, because sorting cases by decades would produce very small numbers of cases for some decades and categories. As it is, the sample sizes for some of the groups are small enough to cause concerns. For Democrats, the number that supported a greater government role is 895, and it is 798 for those who opposed a government role. For Republicans, only 212 supported a government role, and 1,313 opposed a government role. These numbers are small because respondents have to have a party identification, a view about government, the candidate situations they faced, and a vote for the president and the House candidate.

32. Miller and Shanks (1996) also track party identification by cohorts and find that, during the 1960s and the 1970s, the youngest cohort had the lowest identification with parties (pp. 153–159). The difference in their analysis and that presented here is that they attribute the surge in self-defined independent status as a reaction to turmoil in the political system, which is eventually replaced by normalcy. After noting the increase in independents among the youngest during the 1970s, they state "It seems reasonable to conclude that the traumas of the late 1960s and early 1970s—failed presidencies, international frustrations, domestic turmoil, and the disruptive effects of civil rights protests, anti-Vietnam demonstrations, and the countercultural happenings—did initiate a period effect felt throughout the electorate" (p. 155). They later note that "pervasive upturn [in partisanship] since the 1970s has been led by the same young cohorts who were so heavily non-partisan at their original entry into the electorate. As the political climate normalized, the younger cohorts who contributed so much to the apparent national dealignment experienced a dramatic increase in both the incidence and intensity of partisan sentiments in the elections of the 1980s" (p. 158). In their view, the 1960s and 1970s were apparently a reaction to abnormal political system problems. New entrants, who saw many problems not being well addressed by the parties, pulled away from parties in general. As these problems faded in dominance, and some state of "normalcy" returned, these newer entrants into the system became more partisan. The differences between the parties do not matter in this interpretation.

33. The recent increase is puzzling. It involves a relatively small and diminishing sample within the NES data for each year. By 2000, the sample size for the oldest cohort was less than 200, which could result in greater instability of sample estimates. It is unlikely, however, that such a fluctuation would be consistently in one direction. It could be a delayed reaction to the polarization of recent years.

34. To Green et al. (2002), the evidence that there are changes in party identification within panel studies is suspect. Their argument is that party identification is stable, and most of the change we witness is due to measurement error. That is, once we estimate measurement error within panel studies (the studies that track the same individuals over one, two, or four years) and correct for this measurement error, there is no evidence of change. An assessment of the underlying methodology of these analyses is contained in Appendix C: Measurement Error and Partisanship.

35. There is also evidence that some voters have issue differences with their party, but their overall attachment to the party is so strong that they may alter their views to accommodate their party identification. That is, a strong Republican who is uneasy about the positions of the party on cultural issues may gradually move to adopt the views articulated by party elites (Layman and Carsey, 2002a, 2002b).

36. Alternative groupings were tried and the results do not vary. For example, one grouping was those born prior to 1925, 1925–1944, 1945–1964, and 1965 and after. That grouping, as well as others, produced no significant differences in findings.

Bibliography

Abramowitz, Alan I. 1975. "Name Familiarity, Reputation and the Incumbency Effect in a Congressional Election." *Western Political Quarterly,* Vol. 28, No. 4 (December): 668–684.

———. 1989. "Campaigsn Spending in U.S. Senate Elections." *Legislative Studies Quarterly,* Vol. 14, No. 4 (November): 487–507.

———. 1991. "Incumbency, Campaign Spending, and the Decline of Competition in U.S. House Elections." *Journal of Politics,* Vol. 53, No. 1 (February): 34–56.

———. 1994. "Issue Evolution Reconsidered: Racial Attitudes and Partisanship in the U.S. Electorate." *American Journal of Political Science,* Vol. 38, No. 1 (February): 1–24.

Abramowitz, Alan I., and Kyle L. Saunders. 1998. "Ideological Realignments in the U.S. Electorate." *Journal of Politics,* Vol. 60, No. 3 (August): 634–652.

———. 2004. "Rational Hearts and Minds: Social Identity, Ideology, and Party Identification in the American Electorate." Presented at the 2004 American Political Science Association Meetings, Chicago, September 2–5, 2004.

Abramowitz, Alan I., Susan H. Allen, H. Gibbs Knotts, and Kyle L. Saunders. 2002. "Racial Attitudes, Ideology, and the Rise of Republican Identification Among Southern Whites, 1982–2000. Presented at the 2002 American Political Science Association Meetings, Boston, August 30–September 2, 2002.

Adams, Greg D. 1997. "Abortion: Evidence of an Issue Evolution." *American Journal of Political Science.* Vol. 41, No. 3 (July): 718–737.

Aldrich, John. 2003. "Electoral Democracy During Politics as Usual—and Unusual." In Michael B. MacKuen and George Rabinowitz, Editors. *Electoral Democracy.* (Ann Arbor: University of Michigan Press): 279–310.

Alford, John R., and John R. Hibbing. 1981. "Increased Incumbency Advantage in the House." *Journal of Politics,* Vol. 43, No. 4 (November): 1042–1061.

Andersen, Kristi. 1979. *The Creation of a Democratic Majority 1928–1936.* (Chicago: University of Chicago Press).

Ansolabehere, Stephen, James M. Snyder, Jr., and Charles Stewart, III. 2000. "Old Voters, New Voters, and the Personal Vote: Using Redistricting to Measure the Incumbency Advantage." *American Journal of Political Science,* Vol. 44, No. 1 (January): 17–34.

Asher, Herbert. 1974. "Some Consequences of Measurement Error in Survey Data." *American Journal of Political Science,* Vol. 18, No. 2 (May): 469–485.

Bartels, Larry M. 2000. "Partisanship and Voting Behavior, 1952–1996." *American Journal of Political Science,* Vol. 44, No. 1 (January): 35–49.

Bell, Daniel. 1962. The End of Ideology. (New York: Collier Books).

———. 1973. *The Coming of Post-Industrial Society.* (New York: Basic Books).

Benjamin, Gerald, and Michael J. Malbin. 1992. Limiting Legislative Terms. (Washington, D.C.: Congressional Quarterly Press).

Bensel, Richard F. 2000. *The Political Economy of American Industrialism, 1877–1900.* (New York: Cambridge University Press).

Black, Earl, and Merle Black. 1973. "The Demographic Basis of Wallace Support in Alabama." *American Politics Quarterly,* Vol. 1, No. 3 (July): 279–304.

———. 1987. *Politics and Society in the South.* (Cambridge, Mass.: Harvard University Press).

———. 1992. *The Vital South.* (Cambridge, Mass.: Harvard University Press).

———. 2002. *The Rise of Southern Republicans.* (Cambridge, Mass.: Harvard University Press).

Bond, Jon R., and Richard Fleisher, Editors. 2000. *Polarized Politics: Congress and the President in a Partisan Era.* (Washington, D.C.: Congressional Quarterly Press).

Born, Richard. 1979. "Generational Replacement and the Growth of Incumbent Reelection Margins in the U.S. House." *American Political Science Review,* Vol. 73, No. 3 (September): 811–817.

Brady, David W. 1988. *Critical Elections and Congressional Policymaking.* (Stanford, Calif.: Stanford University Press).

Brady, David W., Joseph Cooper, and Patricia A. Hurley. "The Decline of Party in the U.S. House of Representatives, 1887–1968." *Legislative Studies Quarterly* IV, No. 3 (August 1979): 381–407.

Brady, David W., Hahrie Han, and Doug McAdam. 2004. "Party Polarization in the Post-WWII Era: A Two-Period Electoral Interpretation." Presented at the 2004 Midwest Political Science Association Meetings, Chicago, April.

Brennan, Mary C. 1995. *Turning Right in the Sixties: The Conservative Capture of the GOP,* (Chapel Hill: University of North Carolina Press).

Brewer, Mark D. 2004. "A Divided Public? Party Images and Mass Polarization in the United States." *Political Research Quarterly.*

Brewer, Mark D., and Jeffrey M. Stonecash. 2001. "Class, Race Issues, and Declining White Support for the Democratic Party in the South." *Political Behavior,* Vol. 23, No. 2 (June): 131–155.

Broder, David. 1972. The Party's Over: *The Failure of Politics in America.* (New York: Harper & Row).

Buchler, Justin, and Matthew G. Jarvis. 2004. "Split-Ticket Voting and the Realignment of the South." Presented at the 2004 Midwest Political Science Association Meetings, Chicago, April.

Burden, Barry C., and David C. Kimball. 2002. *Why Americans Split Their Tickets: Campaigns, Competition, and Divided Government.* (Ann Arbor: University of Michigan Press).

Burnell, Thomas L., and Bernard Grofman. 1998. "Explaining Divided U.S. Senate Delegations, 1788–1996: A Realignment Approach." *American Political Science Review,* Vol. 92, No. 2 (June): 391–399.

Burner, David. 1968. *The Politics of Provincialism: The Democratic Party in Transition, 1918–1932,* (New York: Alfred A. Knopf).

Burnham, Walter Dean. 1965. "The Changing Shape of the American Political Universe." *American Political Science Review,* Vol. 59, No. 1 (March): 7–28.

———. 1970. *Critical Elections and the Mainsprings of American Politics.* (New York: W.W. Norton).

———. 1975. "Insulation and Responsiveness in Congressional Elections." *Political Science Quarterly,* Vol. 90, No. 3 (Fall): 411–435.

Campaign Finance Institute. 2002. http://www.cfinst.org/studies/vital/commentary.html#noninc.

Campbell, Angus, Philip Converse, Warren Miller, and Donald Stokes. 1960. *The American Voter.* (New York: John Wiley and Sons).

Campbell, James E. 1983. "The Return of the Incumbents: The Nature of the Incumbency Advantage." *Western Political Quarterly,* Vol. 36, No. 3 (September): 434–444.

Carmines, Edward G., and Michael J. Ensley. 2004. "Strengthening and Weakening Mass Partisanship: Issue Preferences and Partisan Attitudes in an Increasingly Polarized Party System." Presented at the 2004 Midwest Political Science Association Meetings, Chicago, April.

Carmines, Edward G., and Harold W. Stanley. 1990. "Ideological Realignment in the Contemporary South: Where Have All the Conservatives Gone?" In Robert P. Steed, Laurence W. Moreland, and Tod A. Baker, editors. *The Disappearing South.* (Tuscaloosa: University of Alabama Press). 21–33.

Carmines, Edward G., and James A. Stimson. 1989. *Issue Evolution: Race and the Transformation of American Politics.* (Princeton, N.J.: Princeton University Press).

Carter, Dan T. 1995. *The Politics of Rage: George Wallace, the Origins of the New Conservatism, and the Transformation of American Politics.* (New York: Simon and Schuster).

Clubb, Jerome M., and Howard W. Allen. 1969. "The Cities and the Election of 1928: Partisan Realignment?" *American Historical Review,* Vol. 74, No. 4 (April): 1205–1220.

Collie, Melissa P. 1981. "Incumbency, Electoral Safety, and Turnover in the House of Representatives, 1972–1976." *American Political Science Review,* Vol. 75, No. 1 (March): 119–131.

Collie, Melissa P., and David W. Brady. 1985. "The Decline of Partisan Voting Coalitions in the House of Representatives." In Lawrence C. Dodd and Bruce I. Oppenheimer, editors, *Congress Reconsidered,* Third Edition. (Washington, D.C.: Congressional Quarterly Press): 272–287.

Congressional Quarterly. 1957. "How Big Is the North-South Democratic Split?" *Congressional Quarterly Almanac.* (Washington, D.C.: Congressional Quarterly, Inc.): 813–817.

———. 1958. "Basic Democratic Divisions Examined." *Congressional Quarterly Almanac.* (Washington, D.C.: Congressional Quarterly, Inc.): 764–769.

———. 1959. "Extent of North-South Democratic Split Analyzed." *Congressional Quarterly Almanac.* (Washington, D.C.: Congressional Quarterly, Inc.): 135–146.

———. 1960. "Extent of North-South Democratic Split Analyzed." *Congressional Quarterly Almanac.* (Washington, D.C.: Congressional Quarterly, Inc.): 117–130.

———. 1961. "Extent of North-South Democratic Split Analyzed." *Congressional Quarterly Almanac.* (Washington, D.C.: Congressional Quarterly, Inc.): 642–657.

———. 1962. "Extent of North-South Democratic Split Analyzed." *Congressional Quarterly Almanac.* (Washington, D.C.: Congressional Quarterly, Inc.). 723–735.

———. 1963. "Extent of North-South Democratic Split Analyzed." *Congressional Quarterly Almanac.* (Washington, D.C.: Congressional Quarterly, Inc.). 740–754.

———. 1964a. "Democrats From North and South Split on 24 % of Votes." *Congressional Quarterly Almanac.* (Washington, D.C.: Congressional Quarterly, Inc.). 745–760.

———. 1964b. Congressional Quarterly's Guide to U.S. Elections, Third Edition. (Washington, D.C.: Congressional Quarterly Press).

———. 1965. "Democrats Regional Divisions Remain Great in 1965." *Congressional Quarterly Almanac.* (Washington, D.C.: Congressional Quarterly, Inc.). 1083–1098.

———. 1966. Representation and Apportionment. (Washington, D.C.: Congressional Quarterly Press).

———. 2001. Congressional Quarterly's Guide to U.S. Elections, Fourth Edition, (Washington, D.C.: Congressional Quarterly Press).

Converse, Philip E. 1976. *The Dynamics of Party Support.* (Beverly Hills, Calif.: Sage).

Cover, Albert D. 1977. "One Good Term Deserves Another: The Advantage of Incumbency in Congressional Elections." *American Journal of Political Science,* Vol. 21, No. 3 (August): 523–542.

Cover, Albert D., and David R. Mayhew. 1977. "Congressional Dynamics and the Decline of Competitive Congressional Elections." In Lawrence C. Dodd and Bruce I. Oppenheimer, editors, *Congress Reconsidered* (Washington, D.C.: CQ Press): 62–82.

Covington, Sally. 1998. "How Conservative Philanthropies and Think Tanks

Transform US Policy." http://www.infoasis.com/www/people/stevetwt/Democracy/ConservThinkTanks.html.

Cox, Gary, and Jonathan Katz. 1996. "Why Did the Incumbency Advantage Grow?" American Journal of Political Science, Vol. 40, No. 2 (May): 478–497.

Crotty, William. 1984. American Parties in Decline. Second Edition. (Boston: Little, Brown, and Co.).

Cummings, Milton C. 1966. Congressmen and the Electorate. (New York: Free Press).

Degler, Carl N. 1964. "American Political Parties and the Rise of the City: An Interpretation." Journal of American History, Vol. 51, No. 1 (June): 41–59.

Derthick, Martha. 1970. The Influence of Federal Grants. (Cambridge, Mass.: Harvard University Press).

Dionne, E.J., Jr. 1997. They Only Look Dead. (New York: Touchstone).

Dreyer, Edward C. 1973. "Change and Stability in Party Identifications." Journal of Politics, Vol. 35, No. 3 (August): 712–722.

Dubin, Michael J. 1998. United States Congressional Elections, 1788–1997. (Jefferson, N.C.: McFarland and Company, Inc.).

Edsall, Thomas Byrne, and Mary D. Edsall. 1991. Chain Reaction: The Impact of Race, Rights, and Taxes on American Politics. (New York: W.W. Norton).

Edwards, Lee. 1999. The Conservative Revolution. (New York: Free Press).

Eldersveld, Samuel J. 1949. "The Influence of Metropolitan Party Pluralities in Presidential Elections Since 1920: A Study of Twelve Key Cities." American Political Science Review, Vol. 43, No. 6 (December): 1189–1206.

Erickson, Robert S. 1971. "The Advantage of Incumbency in Congressional Elections." Polity, Vol. 3, No. 3 (Spring): 395–405.

———. 1972. "Malapportionment, Gerrymandering and Party Fortunes in Congressional Elections." American Political Science Review, Vol. 66, No. 4 (March): 1234–1245.

———. 1976. "Is There Anything Such as a Safe Seat?" Polity, Vol. 8, No. 4 (Summer): 623–632.

Erikson, Robert S., and Gerald C. Wright. 2001. "Voters, Candidates, and Issues in Congressional Elections." In Congress Reconsidered, 7th Edition, Lawrence C. Dodd and Bruce I. Oppenheimer, editors. (Washington, D.C.: Congressional Quarterly Press): 67–95.

Erikson, Robert S., Michael B. MacKuen, and James A. Stimson. 2002. The Macro Polity. (New York: Cambridge University Press).

Ferejohn, John A. 1977. "On the Decline of Competition in Congressional Elections." American Political Science Review, Vol. 71, No. 1 (March): 166–176.

Fiorina, Morris P. 1977. Congress: Keystone to the Washington Establishment. New Haven, Conn.: Yale University Press.

———. 1981a. Retrospective Voting in American National Elections. (New Haven, Conn.: Yale University Press).

———. 1981b. "Some Problems in Studying the Effects of Resource Allocation in Congressional Elections." *American Journal of Political Science*, Vol. 25, No. 3 (August): 543–567.

———. 2002. "Parties and Partisanship: A 40-Year Retrospective." *Political Behavior*, Vol. 24, No. 2 (June): 93–115.

Flanigan, William H., and Nancy H. Zingale. 1979. *Political Behavior of the American Electorate*. 4th Edition. (Boston: Allyn and Bacon).

Fleisher, Richard, and Jon R. Bond. 2000. "Partisanship and the President's Quest for Votes on the Floor of Congress." In Jon R. Bond and Richard Fleisher, Editors, *Polarized Politics: Congress and the President in a Partisan Era*. (Washington, D.C.: Congressional Quarterly Press): 154–185.

———. 2004. "The Shrinking Middle in the US Congress." *British Journal of Political Science*, Vol. 34, Issue 3 (July): 429–451.

Foner, Eric. 1988. *Reconstruction: America's Unfinished Revolution: 1863–1877*. (New York: Cambridge University Press).

Franklin, Charles F. 1992. "Measurement and the Dynamics of Party Identification." *Political Behavior*, Vol. 14, No. 3 (September). 297–309.

Franklin, Charles H., and John E. Jackson. 1983. "The Dynamics of Party Identification." *American Political Science Review*, Vol. 77, No. 4 (December): 957–973.

Garand, James C., and Donald A. Gross. 1984. "Changes in the Vote Margins for Congressional Candidates: A Specification of Historical Trends." *American Political Science Review*, Vol. 78, No. 1 (March): 17–30.

Gardner, Michael. 2002. *Harry Truman and Civil Rights: Moral Courage and Political Risks*. (Carbondale: Southern Illinois University Press).

Glaser, James M. 1996. *Race, Campaign Politics and the Realignment in the South*, (New Haven, Conn.: Yale University Press).

Goodwyn, Lawrence. 1978. *The Populist Moment: A Short History of the Agrarian Revolt in America*. (New York: Oxford University Press).

Green, Donald P. 1991. "The Effects of Measurement Error on Two-Stage, Least Squares Estimates." In James A. Stimson, Editor. *Political Analysis*, Volume 2. (Ann Arbor: University of Michigan Press).

Green, Donald P., and Bradley Palmquist. 1990. "Of Artifacts and Partisan Instability." *American Journal of Political Science*, Vol. 34, No. 3 (August): 872–902.

———. 1994. "How Stable Is Party Identification?" *Political Behavior*. Vol. 16, No. 4. (December): 437–466.

Green, Donald, and Eric Schickler. 1993. "Multiple-Measure Assessment of Party Identification." *Public Opinion Quarterly*, Vol. 57, No. 4 (Winter): 503–535.

Green, Donald P., Bradley Palmquist, and Eric Shickler. 2002. *Partisan Hearts and Minds: Political Parties and the Social Identities of Voters*. (New Haven, Conn.: Yale University Press).

Green, John C., Lyman A. Kellstedt, Corwin E. Smidt, and James L. Guth. 1998. "The Soul of the South: Religion and the New Electoral Order." In Charles S. Bullock III and Mark J. Rozell, *The New Politics of the Old South*. (Boulder, Colo.: Rowman and Littlefield): 261–276.

Grofman, Bernard, William Koetzle, Michael McDonald, and Thomas Brunell.

2000. "A New Look at Split-Ticket Outcomes for House and President: The Comparative Midpoints Model." *Journal of Politics,* Vol. 62, No. 1 (February): 34–50.

Groseclose, Tim, Steven D. Levitt, and James M. Snyder, Jr. 1999. "Comparing Interest Group Scores Across Time and Chambers: Adjusted ADA Scores for the U.S. Congress." *American Political Science Review,* Vol. 93, No. 1 (March): 33–50.

Hale, Jon F. 1995. "The Making of the New Democrats." *Political Science Quarterly,* Vol. 110, No. 2: 207–232.

Hays, Samuel. 1964. "The Politics of Reform in Municipal Government," Pacific Northwest Quarterly, Vol. 55, No. 4 (October): 157–169.

Heise, David R. 1969. "Separating Reliability and Stability in Test-Retest Correlation." *American Sociological Review,* Vol. 34, No. 1 (February): 93–101.

———. 1998. *Congressional Elections: Campaigning at Home and in Washington,* (Washington, D.C.: Congressional Quarterly Press).

Hetherington, Marc J. 2001. "Resurgent Mass Partisanship: The Role of Elite Polarization?" *American Political Science Review,* Vol. 95, No. 3 (September): 619–632.

Hodgson, Godfrey. 1996. *The World Turned Right Side Up.* (Boston: Mariner Books).

Hofstader, Richard. 1955. *The Age of Reform* (New York: Vintage).

Inglehart, Ronald. 1971. "The Silent Revolution in Europe." *American Political Science Review,* Vol. 65, No. 4 (December): 991–1017.

———. 1977. *Silent Revolution.* (Princeton, N.J.: Princeton University Press).

———. 1997. *Modernization and Postmodernization.* (Princeton, N.J.: Princeton University Press).

Jackson, John E. 1975. "Issues, Party Choices, and Presidential Votes." *American Journal of Political Science,* Vol. 19, No. 2 (May): 161–185.

Jacobson, Gary C. 2000. "Party Polarization in National Politics: The Electoral Connection." In *Polarized Politics: Congress and the President in a Partisan Era,* Jon R. Bond and Richard Fleisher, Editors. (Washington, D.C.: Congressional Quarterly Press): 9–30.

———. 2001. *The Politics of Congressional Elections.* 5th edition. (New York: Addison Wesley Longman).

———. 2003a. "Party Polarization in Presidential Support: The Electoral Connection." *Congress and the Presidency.* Vol. 30, No. 1 (Spring): 1–36.

———. 2003b. "Reconsidering 'Reconsidering the Trend in Incumbent Vote Percentages in House Elections': A Comment." *The American Review of Politics,* Vol. 24: 241–244.

———. 2004. "Explaining the Ideological Polarization of the Congressional Parties Since the 1970s." Presented at the 2004 Midwest Political Science Association Meetings, Chicago, April.

James, Scott C. 2000. *Presidents, Parties, and the State.* (Cambridge, UK: Cambridge University Press).

Johannes, John R., and John C. McAdams. 1981. "The Congressional

Incumbency Effect: Is It Casework, Policy Compatibility, or Something Else?" *American Journal of Political Science,* Vol. 25, No. 3 (August): 512–542.

Jones, Charles O. 1964. "Inter-Party Competition in Congressional Seats." *Western Political Quarterly,* Vol. 17, No. 3 (September): 461–476.

Keith, Bruce E., David B. Magleby, Candice J. Nelson, Elizabeth Orr, Mark C. Westlye, Raymond Wolfinger. 1992. *The Myth of the Independent Voter.* (Berkeley: University of California Press).

Key, V.O., Jr. 1949. *Southern Politics in State and Nation.* (New York: Knopf).

———. 1955. "A Theory of Critical Elections." *Journal of Politics,* Vol. 17, No. 1 (February): 3–18.

———. 1959. "Secular Realignment and the Party System." *Journal of Politics,* Vol. 21, No. 2 (May): 198–210.

Kousser, J. Morgan. 1974. *The Shaping of Southern Politics: Suffrage Restriction and the Establishment of the One-Party South, 1880–1910.* (New Haven, Conn.: Yale University Press).

Krasno, Jonathon S., and Donald P. Green. 1988. "Preempting Quality Challengers in House Elections." *Journal of Politics,* Vol. 50, No 4 (November): 920–936.

Krehbiel, Keith, and John R. Wright. 1983. "The Incumbency Effect in Congressional Elections: A Test of Two Explanations." *American Journal of Political Science,* Vol. 27, No. 1 (February): 140–157.

Ladd, Everett Carll and Charles Hadley. 1975. *Transformations of the American Party System.* (New York: W.W. Norton).

Layman, Geoffrey C. 1999. "'Cultural Wars' in the American Party System." *American Politics Quarterly,* Vol. 27, No. 1 (January): 89–121.

———. 2001. *The Great Divide: Religious and Cultural Conflict in American Party Politics.* (New York: Columbia University Press).

Layman, Geoffrey C., and Thomas M. Carsey. 2002a. "Party Polarization and Party Structuring of Policy Attitudes: A Comparison of Three NES Panel Studies." *Political Behavior,* Vol. 24, No. 3 (September): 199–236.

———. 2002b. "Party Polarization and "Conflict Extension" in the American Electorate." *American Journal of Political Science,* Vol. 46, No. 4 (October): 786–802.

Leege, David C., Kenneth D. Wald, Brian S. Krueger, and Paul D. Mueller. 2002. *The Politics of Cultural Differences.* (Princeton, N.J.: Princeton University Press).

Lemann, Nicholas. 1991. *The Promised Land.* (New York: Knopf).

Levitt, Steven D., and Catherine D. Wolfram. 1997. "Decomposing the Sources of Incumbency Advantage." *Legislative Studies Quarterly,* Vol. 22, No. 1 (February): 45–60.

Lubell, Samuel. 1956. *The Future of American Politics.* 2nd ed., Revised. Garden City, N.Y.: Doubleday Anchor Books.

Macdonald, Stuart Elain, George Rabinowitz, and Holly Brasher. 2003. "Policy Issues and Electoral Democracy." In Michael B. MacKuen and George Rabinowitz, Editors. *Electoral Democracy.* (Ann Arbor: University of Michigan Press). 172–199.

MacKeun, Michael B., Robert S. Erikson, and James A. Stimson. 1989. "Macropartisanship." *American Political Science Review,* Vol. 83, No. 4 (December): 1125–1142.

MacKeun, Michael B., Robert S. Erikson, James A. Stimson, and Kathleen Knight. 2003. "Elections and the Dynamics of Ideological Representation." In Michael B. MacKuen and George Rabinowitz, editors, *Electoral Democracy.* (Ann Arbor: University of Michigan Press). 200–237.

Magnet, Myron. 1993. *The Dream and the Nightmare: The Sixties Legacy to the Underclass.* (New York: William Morrow).

Martis, Kenneth C., 1982. *The Historical Atlas of U.S. Congressional Districts, 1789–1983.* (New York: The Free Press).

Mayhew, David R. 1974a. *The Electoral Connection.* (New Haven, Conn.: Yale University Press).

———. 1974b. "Congressional Elections: The Case of the Vanishing Marginals." *Polity,* Vol. 6: 295–317.

———. 2003. *Electoral Realignments: A Critique of an American Genre.* (New Haven, Conn.: Yale University Press).

Menefee-Libey, David. 2000. *The Triumph of Candidate-Centered Politics.* (New York: Chatham House).

Mettler, Suzanne B. 1998. *Dividing Citizens: Gender and Federalism in New Deal Public Policy.* (Ithaca, N.Y.: Cornell University Press).

Miller, Warren E., and J. Merrill Shanks. 1996. *The New American Voter.* (Cambridge, Mass.: Harvard University Press).

Murray, Charles. 1984. *Losing Ground.* (New York: Basic Books).

Nelson, Candice J. 1978–1979. "The Effect of Incumbency on Voting in Congressional Elections." *Political Science Quarterly,* Vol. 93, No. 4 (Winter): 665–678.

Nie, Norman, Sidney Verba and John Petrocik. 1976. *The Changing American Voter* (Cambridge, Mass.: Harvard University Press).

Palmer, John L., and Isabel V. Sawhill, Editors. 1982. *The Reagan Experiment.* (Washington, D.C.: The Urban Institute Press).

———. 1984. *The Reagan Record.* (Cambridge, Mass.: Ballinger Publishing).

Parker, Glenn R. 1980. "The Advantage of Incumbency in House Elections." *American Politics Quarterly,* Vol. 8, No. 4 (October): 449–464.

Patterson, Thomas E. 2002. *The Vanishing Voter: Public Involvement in an Age of Uncertainty.* (New York: Knopf).

Paulson, Arthur C. 2000. *Realignment and Party Revival: Understanding American Electoral Politics at the Turn of the Twenty-First Century.* (Westport, Conn.: Praeger).

Payne, James L. 1980. "The Personal Electoral Advantage of House Incumbents, 1936–1976." *American Politics Quarterly,* Vol. 8, No. 4 (October): 465–482.

Perlstein, Rick. 2001. *Before the Storm.* (New York: Hill and Wang).

Polsby, Nelson. 1968. "The Institutionalization of the House of Representatives." *American Political Science Review,* Vol. 62, No. 1 (March): 144–168.

————. 2004. *How Congress Evolves: Social Bases of Institutional Change.* (New York: Oxford University Press).

Pomper, Gerald M. 1972. "From Confusion to Clarity: Issues and American Voters, 1956–1968." *American Political Science Review,* Vol. 66, No. 2 (June): 415–428.

Poole, Keith T., and Howard Rosenthal. 1984. "The Polarization of American Politics." *Journal of Politics,* Vol. 46, No. 4 (November): 1061–1079.

————. 1985. "A Spatial Model for Legislative Roll Call Analysis." *American Journal of Political Science,* Vol. 29, No. 2 (May): 357–384.

————. 1991. "Patterns of Congressional Voting." *American Journal of Political Science,* Vol. 35, No. 1 (February): 228–278.

————. 1997. *Congress: A Political-Economic History of Roll Call Voting.* (New York: Oxford University Press).

Popkin, Samuel L. 1994. *The Reasoning Voter: Communication and Persuasion in Presidential Elections.* (Chicago: University of Chicago Press).

Rae, Nicol C. 1989. *The Decline and Fall of the Liberal Republicans from 1952 to the Present.* (New York: Oxford University Press).

Reiter, Howard L. 2001. "The Building of a Bifactional Structure: The Democrats in the 1940s." *Political Science Quarterly,* Vol. 116, No. 1 (Spring): 107–129.

Ricci, David. 1993. *The Transformation of American Politics: The New Washington and the Rise of Think Tanks.* (New Haven, Conn.: Yale University Press).

Roberts, Jason M., and Steven S. Smith. 2003. "Procedural Contexts, Party Strategy, and Conditional Party Voting in the U.S. House of Representatives, 1971–2000." *American Journal of Political Science,* Vol. 47, No. 2 (April): 305–317.

Rohde, David W. 1991. *Parties and Leaders in the Postreform House.* (Chicago: University of Chicago Press).

Rusk, Jerrold G. 2001. *A Statistical History of the American Electorate.* (Washington, D.C.: Congressional Quarterly Press).

Sanders, Elizabeth. 1999. *Roots of Reform: Farmers, Workers, and the American State.* (Chicago: University of Chicago Press).

Schlesinger, Arthur M., Jr. 1957. *Crisis of the Old Order.* (Boston: Houghton Mifflin.)

Schreckhise, William D., and Todd G. Shields. 2003. "Ideological Realignment in the Contemporary U.S. Electorate Revisited." *Social Science Quarterly,* Vol. 84, No. 3 (September): 596–612.

Serra, George. 1994. "What's in It for Me? The Impact of Congressional Casework on Incumbent Evaluation." *American Politics Quarterly,* Vol. 22, No. 4 (October): 403–420.

Serra, George, and Albert D. Cover. 1992. "The Electoral Consequences of Perquisite Use: The Casework Case." *Legislative Studies Quarterly,* Vol. 17, No. 2 (May): 233–246.

Shafer, Byron E., et al., 1991. *The End of Realignment? Interpreting American Electoral Eras.* (Madison: University of Wisconsin Press).

Shively, W. Philips. 1980. "The Nature of Party Identification: A Review of

Recent Developments." In John C. Piece and John L. Sullivan, Editors, *The Electorate Reconsidered.* (Beverly Hills, Calif.: Sage).

———. 1992. "From Differential Abstention to Conversion: A Change in Electoral Change, 1864–1988." *American Journal of Political Science,* Vol. 36, No. 2 (May): 309–330.

Stanley, Harold W., and Richard G. Niemi. 2001. *Vital Statistics on American Politics, 2001–2002.* (Washington, D.C.: Congressional Quarterly Press).

Stefancic, Jean, and Richard Delgado. 1997. *No Mercy: How Conservative Think Tanks and Foundations Changed America's Social Agenda.* (Philadelphia: Temple University Press).

Stonecash, Jeffrey M. 1993. "The Pursuit and Retention of Legislative Office in New York, 1870–1990: Reconsidering Sources of Change." *Polity,* Vol. 26, No. 2 (Winter): 301–315.

———. 2000. *Class and Party in American Politics.* (Boulder, Colo.: Westview Press).

———. 2002. "The Double-Edged Sword: Party Dilemmas in Mobilizing Electoral Bases in U.S. House Elections." John Green and John Freeman, editors, *The State of the Parties.* (Lanham, Md.: Rowman and Littlefield).

———. 2003a. "Reconsidering the Trend in Incumbent Vote Percentages in House Elections." *American Review of Politics,* Vol. 24 (Fall): 225–239.

———. 2003b. "Response to Jacobson's Comments." *American Review of Politics,* Vol. 24 (Fall): 245–248.

Stonecash, Jeffrey M., Mark D. Brewer, and Mack D. Mariani. 2002. "Northern Democrats and Polarization in the U.S. House." *Legislative Studies Quarterly,* Vol. 27, No. 3 (August): 423–444.

———. 2003. *Diverging Parties: Social Change, Realignment, and Party Polarization.* (Boulder, Colo.: Westview Press).

Stonecash, Jeffrey M., and Everita Silina. 2005. "Reassessing the 1896 Realignment." *American Political Research,* Vol. 33, No. 1 (January): 3–32.

Stonecash, Jeffrey M., and Amy Widestrom. 2004. "The Post-WWII Decline in the Incumbency Effect." Presented at the 2004 Northeast Political Science Association Meetings, Boston, November.

Sundquist, James L. 1983. *Dynamics of the Party System: Alignment and Realignment of Political Parties in the United States,* Revised Edition. (Washington, D.C.: Brookings Institution).

Turner, Julius. 1949. "Voting Behavior in the House of Representatives: A Study of Representative Government and Political Pressure." Dissertation, Johns Hopkins University, Baltimore, Md.

———. 1951. *Party and Constituency: Pressures on Congress.* The Johns Hopkins University Studies in Historical and Political Science, Series 69, No. 1. (Baltimore, Md.: The Johns Hopkins Press).

Turner, Julius, and Edward V. Schneier. 1970. *Party and Constituency: Pressures on Congress,* Revised Edition. (Baltimore, Md.: Johns Hopkins Press).

U.S. Bureau of the Census. 1945. "Population of the United States by

Congressional Districts." Population-Special Reports. Series p-45, No. 6. July 3. (Washington, D.C.: U.S. Government Printing Office). 1–2.

U.S. Bureau of the Census. 1957. *County and City Data Book 1956.* "Appendix G: Selected Data for Congressional Districts." (Washington, D.C.: U.S. Government Printing Office): 495–512.

U.S. Bureau of the Census. 1961. *Congressional District Data Book (Districts of the 87th Congress)*—A Statistical Abstract Supplement. (Washington, D.C.: U.S. Government Printing Office).

U.S. Bureau of the Census. 1963. *Congressional District Data Book (Districts of the 88th Congress)*—A Statistical Abstract Supplement. (Washington, D.C.: U.S. Government Printing Office).

U.S. Bureau of the Census. 1983. Congressional District Prifiles, 98th Congress: Supplementary Report PC80-S1-11, September. (Washington, D.C.: U.S. Government Printing Office).

Ware, Alan. 2002. *The American Direct Primary: Party Institutionalization and Transformation in the North.* (New York: Cambridge University Press).

Wattenberg, Martin P. 1990. *The Decline of American Political Parties, 1952–1988.* (Cambridge, Mass.: Harvard University Press).

———. 1991. *The Rise of Candidate-Centered Politics.* (Cambridge, Mass.: Harvard University Press).

Weatherford, M. Stephen. 1978. "Economic Conditions and Electoral Outcomes: Class Differences in the Political Response to Recession." *American Journal of Political Science,* Vol. 22, No. 4 (November): 917–938.

White, John K. 2003. *The Values Divide: American Politics and Culture in Transition.* (New York: Chatham House).

Wiebe, Robert. 1967. *The Search for Order, 1877–1920.* (New York: Hill and Wang).

Wiley, David E., and James A. Wiley. 1970. "The Estimation of Measurement Error in Panel Data." *American Sociological Review,* Vol. 35, No. 1 (February). 112–117.

Yiannakis, Diana Evans. 1981. "The Grateful Electorate: Casework and Congressional Elections." *American Journal of Political Science,* Vol. 25, No. 3 (August): 568–580.

Index

About the Book

After years of decline, why has party attachment become a strong force once again in U.S. politics? Jeffrey Stonecash argues that the recent resurgence of partisanship is but the latest chapter in a larger story of party realignment—a story that reaffirms the centrality of political parties.

Stonecash marshals rich data from more than a century of elections to highlight unexpected patterns of voting behavior with key significance today. As party constituencies continue to reorganize, he contends convincingly, the United States will face the strengthening of party attachments and growing political polarization.

Jeffrey M. Stonecash is professor of political science at Syracuse University. His publications include *Class and Party in American Politics* and *Political Polling*.